Thresholds

&

Testimonies

Thresholds & Testimonies

Recovering Order in
Literature and Criticism
Volume one of The Fall and the Gods

FREDERIC WILL

WAYNE STATE UNIVERSITY PRESS   DETROIT   1988

Author Acknowledgments
University House, at the University of Iowa, has supported the
work with every courtesy; for which I warmly thank Jay Semel and
Lorna Olson. I am indebted to Fred van der Zee of Editions Rodopi
in Amsterdam, for permission to reprint, in altered form, "The
Argument of Water," which first appeared in *Belphagor* in 1977. "The
Quanta of Imagination" appeared, in wholly different form, in *The
Fact of Literature* (Rodopi, 1973).

Library of Congress Cataloging-in-Publication Data

Will, Frederic.
    Thresholds and testimonies.

    (The fall and the gods ; v. 1)
    Bibliography: p.
    Includes index.
    1. Literature—Philosophy.   2. Literature—Translations
into foreign languages—History and criticism.
3. Poetry—Philosophy.   4. Poetry—Translations into
foreign languages—History and criticism.   I. Title.
II. Title: Thresholds and testimonies.   III. Series: Will,
Frederic.   Fall and the gods ; v. 1.
PN49.W55 1988   801   88-145
ISBN 0-8143-1943-2 (alk. paper)

Grateful acknowledgment is made to the publishers of the
following poems for permission to quote in full. Gary
Snyder, "A Walk." From *The Back Country*. Copyright
© 1968 by Gary Snyder. Reprinted by permission of New
Directions Publishing Corporation. Wallace Stevens, "The
Glass of Water." From The Collected Works of Wallace
Stevens. Copyright © 1957 by Wallace Stevens. Reprinted
by permission of Alfred A. Knopf, Inc.

Grateful acknowledgment is made to the University of Iowa for
financial assistance in the publication of this volume.

The inmost identity of I and God, underlying everything, is simply an expression of the proposition: like is conceivable only by like.

Bonhoeffer, *Act and Being*

The gift is not merely the witness or guardian to new life, but the creator.

Hyde, *The Gift*

Ne cherche pas les limites de la mer. Tu les détiens. Elles te sont offertes au même instant que ta vie évaporée.

René Char, *Le Rempart de Brindilles*

Liminality has been likened to death, to being in the womb, to invisibility, to darkness, to bisexuality, to the wilderness, and to an eclipse of the sun or moon.

Turner, *The Ritual Process*

Contents

Preface

In the following volume—the first in a trilogy—I lean to that order of things the great religions affirm. I see such order where junctions form between adjacent and yet nonidentical planes of experience, at thresholds between, say, texts in different languages, seemingly discrepant scientific and poetic ways of accounting for experience, or between the recoverable and the seemingly lost portions of our cultural heritage. At junctures between such discrepant zones we signal our recuperative pleasure—do so in testimonies or in the widest sense translations; we testify to our discovery in writing or thought or silent awareness.

The first and last essays—on translation and testifying, respectively—indicate the argument of *Thresholds and Testimonies*. The first essay—on untranslatability—makes a simply logical claim; that untranslatability can never be proven—between texts no matter how alien to one another—and could only be claimed in the process of translation. (The formula of wider application is that unintelligibility can never be proven because only the intelligible could prove it.) The last essay deals with testimony to such translation process, and to examples of it taken from the aesthetic, moral, and cognitive spheres. The dynamic here is of convergence, and the stress is on normative values. The realm of the beautiful is brought into existence by perceiving acts, in which we cross over into the formerly unfamiliar text or sculpture or sonata, disclosing it and ourselves simultaneously. The ethical norm is generated by loving awareness of continuity among our kind, while at some points we have been *its* to one another. Threshold crossings provoke those works or acts or realizations in which we find the existence of value confirmed.

The perspectives of the first and last essay reoccur elsewhere here, but against very different backgrounds.

The second essay deals with the ontological background inside which beauty finds its actuality. My concern is with the genesis of sculptural works from nature's raw state—at the touch of the human artist. I take as my understanding-grid, through which to watch the birth of a Phidian head, a universe that is by nature one and made of spirit. (The historical model is a Plotinian monism, and the conduct of my argument like that of Plotinus in the *Enneads*.) I see the beautiful emerging in sculpture from a desire in nature—to be more self-identically the spirit potential to it—a desire which meets, in the maieutic of the higher-spirit sculptor, with the beauty of the sculptured head. Continuity in being is the field for a series of threshold transitions—of matter upward through itself into its own expressiveness, of sculptor down into matter and upward with matter across its threshold into art—which resemble those effected by the translator. Essay three—prose poems in illustration—smears actuality across the argument.

The essays (two and three) in question just now are concerned with synchronic events, with the way consciousness works. At the center of the book lie two long essays dealing with separate languages which converge into one another through their common statements—thus in effect translating themselves into one another across thresholds.

"The Argument of Water" examines texts concerning water taken from religious, poetic, and scientific discourse. (I turn to ancient Buddhist and Christian texts, some work from Eliot and René Char, and some early modern science—Newton, Gassendi, Boyle—and in each case hunt for the distinctive language applied to an account of water.) My conclusion is that all these types of discourse are different—but only as different ways of doing the same work; that they cross thresholds into one another at the point where their common themes substantiate them.

"The Quanta of Imagination" juxtaposes two differently accented accounts of what the imagination is and does. Here there is no single theme like water to anchor the displays. I follow Coleridge (on the one hand) and certain recent language analysts (on the other) into different thought-lines, concluding that the latter group amassed a huge anthology of Romantic-Coleridgean views of the way imagination works. My stress here is on intersecting aesthetics, which find each other from different languages and premises about language, and constitute mutual thresholds for one another.

Essay seven, "Limits in the Time of Consciousness," points similar thoughts into a diachronic zone, yet even so—as my lone historical essay—it evokes the antitemporal element in the experience of history. I am concerned with the limitations of our consciousness, in its odyssey of recovering the cultural past within it. The perspective is that of a contemporary Western Psyche, but I cast present consciousness backward—through confrontation with ancient sites like Kuaua (in New Mexico) or Effigy Mounds (in Iowa) and through texts from Gary Snyder, Alfred de Vigny, Angelus Silesius, François Villon, Horace, and Sappho. I find the farther past increasingly resistant, yet my point is that nothing emerges from within the reading of that past which is able to disprove or even cast doubt on its readability. Again we face the first essay's logical conundrum and mystery. The cultural past refuses to refuse itself to its archaeologists, though the continuity it guarantees them is only as rich as the detail and accuracy with which they have opened it. Each threshold, before each deeper interior room, is a door of testimony across which we march, reaching through it with our eyes and minds.

Essay six, the essay on the essay, surveys the development of the genre through excerpts from Montaigne, Addison and Steele, Lamb, Pater, Tom Wolfe, and others. This quasi history displays the timeless physiognomy of the essay's work. The genre's stance is on the one hand immediacy to the world to be described, and on the other art, craft, and form. This intermediate position is the essay's openness to other forms which circumscribe it and which it in turn helps to define. The essay lives as testimony to the thresholds which are its opening out, and the remaining genre-world's opening in toward it.

This essay is the threshold from which I cross into all the

remaining pieces—on thresholds among the continuous domains of experience. The essay itself is the microcosmic instance of such continuity, the cross-over point at which art forms and colloquial utterance meet.

First volume in a trilogy, *Thresholds and Testimonies* establishes leitmotifs for its succession: *A Portrait of John* and *Founding the Lasting*. Both those works reflect a world in which order is implicit—even in disorder. Both relate order to continuity, and continuity to details of sequence. The second volume, *A Portrait of John,* traces these motifs through an individual life—that of a close friend of the author. Thus it shows rather than argues the point of the trilogy. The third volume, *Founding the Lasting,* carries the larger argument into two fresh channels: looking at man's fallen condition and the imaginative curiosity of return it has bred in us; and seeing how that curiosity works itself out into the ontology and history of literary art. All three volumes rest under the larger title, *The Fall and the Gods;* for all three model the freshness that marks our endless rejuvenation in the face of death.

Untranslatability

All things are an equal exchange for fire and fire for all things.
Heraclitus

I found my way into translation through Kostes Palamas' long lyric *The Palm Tree:* American School of
Classical Studies, Speusippou Street, Athens, 1952.
Sun on a text—itself an unpromising pathetic fallacy in early twentieth century *demotike*—about an oasis palm tree and the jubilant
flowers that one spring morning wake to life at its feet. The flowers
address the tree, shamelessly blessing their life and that of the lord
above them. Reading this poem I was overwhelmed by sadness,
happiness, and intricate interest and started to try to make English
of these lines, which were as profoundly un-English as was the
conduct of their argument. An electric shock crossed me that was
the inception of a several-year project, ultimately of translating and
remaking two epics by Palamas; and this shock was before all a
seizure by the chemistry of testifying, of raising a hand in my own
language—in the presence of a potent voice in another language.
I take it—but am guessing—that translators would often give
similar accounts of their discovery of affinity. The chemistry would
vary in each instance, but something in the language of testifying
should be there.

What about the negative aspect? Some texts are uncongenial
to some translators. Personally, I could translate *Les liaisons dan-*

I

gereuses by Choderlos de Laclos but not *Les misérables,* because the former is—for me—a rich aesthetic surface with a lot of self-interested fascinations, while the latter is talky and inefficient. I feel myself at stake in the Laclos. Another person—with an eye to the build of narrative—might prefer taking on Victor Hugo. He or she might find Laclos untranslatable. Gregory Rabassa finds himself drawn to translate the grand Latin American novel, but who wants him to translate Herondas? He couldn't do it. Or imagine Pope translating Sappho. There is obviously a kind of translatability deriving from individual traits and differences. We can only go so far beyond what we are.

Are some texts—above and beyond the matter of individual affinity, of testifying and chemistry—absolutely over the brink, unreachable? Can some texts not be brought back into sight by any translator, even by the well-intentioned feeler of affinity? Or is untranslatability in this absolute sense nonexistent? Can everything be translated?

I don't think there is such a thing as absolute untranslatability. Proving, or at least arguing, that interests me for reasons that extend beyond the purpose of this first essay, though it is this essay's main point. I will later be going from discussion of translation to discussion of other threshold-meeting situations, passages into new forms like perception (after sensation), self-awareness (after mere coexistence with oneself), or life (after death). I will be going into liminal issues, posing the questions of whether a variety of meaning-code barriers can be interpreted, penetrated, and transcended—yielding the unexpected and new. Translation will serve as an introductory model for remarks on these situations.

First, I will take a little poem by Heine, then a snatch attributed to the young Plato, then a Copper Eskimo dance-song, then a piece of Manx. Of each of these (difficult to translate) pieces I will be asking, Can it be translated? Or is it, in the difficulties it will obviously occasion, an example of the untranslatable?

Das Fräulein stand am Meere
und seufzte lang und bang.
Es rührte sie so sehre
Der Sonnenuntergang.

Mein Fräulein, sein Sie munter,
Das ist ein altes Stück;
Hier vorne geht sie unter
Und kehrt von hinten zurück.[1]

Specimen 1
Upon this shore, a maiden
sighs with a troubled frown;
she seems so sorrow-laden
to see the sun go down.

Don't let the old thing grieve you,
look up and smile, my dear;
for though in front he may leave you,
he'll rise again in the rear.

(Translated by Untermeyer, 1917)

Specimen 2
The maid looked over the ocean
and sighed with a worried frown;
she sighed with deep emotion
because the sun went down.

Dear girl, don't let it grieve you,
it's an old trick, you will find;
In front he sinks, to leave you
and come again from behind.

(Translated by Draper, 1982)

Specimen 3
Ocean lies like a frown on her face, sunset falling into the gulf below her.
She sighs. Passages of old texts move her. Can she not grow lighter, can
she not remember: fiery balls return from the rear?

(Translated by F. Will, 1985)

By conventional perspective—of time, place, and circumstance—
this Heine text might seem the most accessible of my examples.

The world condition from which he writes is continuous with ours. It is 1832. The author has just returned from a first trip to Paris—has seen the new bourgeoisie, us, in action; he has found a political ideology, Saint-Simonisme—characterized in section 7 of *Sera-phine;* he is sharpening his teeth in and against a Romantic mode that we still know intimately, if often in self-hatred. What should be unavailable to us in a Western European perspective of this recent vintage? And so forth. Yet some of the barriers to translation in the present instance are high and glass-spiked. Romantic irony—what we call Heine's strategy here—tortures us today with a close-ness we cannot quite reach. (We can be bitter, black humorous, Romantic—as was e e cummings; but we falter at Heine's bump-tiously dark tone. Even Roethke falters there. Yet the awareness of that faltering is evidence of closeness, of a near miss. For how else would we know that we did not know the Heine mode?) Further-more, we are stumped by the prosody, the form-expression that fits the poem's teasing irony, its self-mocking jocularity. How can we make contemporary English of it?

Untermeyer and Draper move heavily from formal hints, with predictably archaic results. (Even Untermeyer's old effort in the second decade of the century was contemporary with the revolution in modern U.S. poetry—with *Poetry,* with Pound. But he pays no attention. Translation against one's time-grain almost never works.) Both translators overcompensate with sexual references at the end, for their only teetering sense of Heine's balance—poised as it is between cosmology and the off-color. Will—offering him-self as his own victim—substitutes new risks of extrinsic form loss, of gross tone-change, in order to testify (as he temporarily sees it) honestly. (Honesty is a complex criterion here, yet the first one Will wants to rehabilitate. Rawly put, honesty in Will's translation means to him writing what he could say without feeling denatured, without blushing aloud. But this formulation is simplistically pri-vate, for the translator's language-nature, that to which his honesty must be true, is formed by his whole milieu. It is an artificial nature in which he has come to feel perfectly natural, as a writer feels in his style.) What Will hopes to achieve is a slice of approximation, an angle. (Long ago, he thinks, he considered such approximations efforts to express an idea-nexus that lay equally beyond and outside them and the original. For his thinking at that stage, the original had no privileged claim on expressing its nexus, its point, which was equally expressible by translations of that original. Now he sees it a little differently. The original seems to him to be its idea, or point, more indissolubly than he had figured. Translations appear to him handicapped in their effort to emulate originals, to include their argument in their form. Handicapped but not gelded.) Will's slice of approximation, like Untermeyer's, raises the question of the moment.

Is Heine's poem translatable? Do these three failure-examples suggest that a fourth, a right fourth, might succeed, might be it? Or do they start toward proof that Heine's fragment could never be put into English? I have already said that I do not believe in untranslatability—in letters or in life. Let me illustrate in terms of an attitude toward culture. It seems to me that culture exists as repeated approximations of the natural—the natural spontaneous, the cosmic element that shades off into it—and that nature exists itself as the possibility of culture. I would even go further and see evidence that the inorganic-organic relationships set a precedent for the nature-culture relation. From the inorganic to culture there is a mutually sensitive continuum. Heine's text and translations of it seem to me to exist in some such kind of mutual interimplication. Or rather, what Heine's text means stands in mutually approximating sets of relationships to Heine's text itself and to the translations of it. In such mutuality zones, texts and their translations refuse any intermittent barrier that is not a way of keeping them more conscious of one another, more aware of ways of stating one another.

Another way to look at it: the central way. The only proof of untranslatability would have to be amassed by working and thinking through sets of translations, by translating. But nothing in that thinking could prove the ultimate impotence of that thinking and working. The dilemma would be like the effort to establish unintelligibility. I can go up to it—to the undecodable hieroglyph, the Easter Island giant—with unintelligibility, but I cannot know it except as the intelligible. I cannot know that I cannot know Cambodian or quantum physics, except in terms of what I am able to know of them.

Ancient Hellenic tradition attributed to Plato the following fragment of longing:

astér prín men elámpes
ení zooísin heóos
nún de, thanón,
lámpeis Hésperos
én phthimenoís

From the first—chapter 10, Chase and Phillips, *Introduction to Greek*—this fragment stunned me and sent a prep school brat away eery. I still repeat it when life is trying to demystify itself.

Star formerly you used to shine
among the living as a dawn star
But now, having died,   .
you shine like Hesperos among the worn away

Transliterated, literalized, the text suffers from more than usual blood loss. The original art is all in the suppression of artifice, the making itself so natural that no part of it catches, while all belongs to itself. The literal . . . well. Others, like Willis Barnstone, have tried lifting it:

You were the morning star among the living.
In death, O Evening Star, you light the dead.

(Translated by Barnstone, 1962)

But anybody could do that. All you need is a dictionary and a free half hour. And then to your amazement you remember the kind of translation at which at first you think, Perfect: it had to be. Shelley's prefatory emblem to *Adonais* (1812):

Thou wert the morning-star among the living,
Ere thy fair light had fled;
Now, having died, thou art as Hesperus, giving
New splendour to the dead.

Time alone hacks at such greatness and forces Will—like other fools—to add,

System-immune you caught on the sun,
life in your face,
then died like deer,
fetlock tufts felty,
beauty's wind your words.

The heart of my argument is that untranslatability is a nonconcept, can never be proven; yet now I hear the hard corollary: even seemingly perfect translation cannot exist, must yield to time. Stasis is not allowed. All things flow. Shelley went close to the fire. In some sense this (alleged) Plato fragment yielded to him, and proved itself more accessible to people like us than Heine's quatrains. In this Plato lyric there is a less local mode-tone than in Heine, none of Heine's complex compacting of what Schiller called the naive and sentimental modes (spontaneity plus innocence on the one hand; on the other, sophisticated nostalgia). Yet this Platonic frag-ment—like the best Hellenic lyrics, in Archilochos and Bacchyl-ides—proves purer and simpler than Shelley's naming equipment. (Ancient Greek lyric at its finest is like that purest water from the center of the spring, to which Winckelmann compared the ideal beauty of Apolline statuary.) Shelley's additions of *fair* and *splen-dour* mar what, in its perfect sound valence, became in Plato total freedom from excess. Plato's "light" is not "fair," nor need it be, so named as it is with beauty for its aureole. Plato's beloved gives no "new splendours" to the dead; for his mere existence there, without statement, includes its splendor. Shelley's minima betray him, at work overlarding the ancient.

Neither Heine nor Plato is untranslatable, nor perfectly—that is, genuinely—translatable. I am sharpening the former point— the emptiness of the class *untranslatable*—because in the end I want that point to penetrate a variety of limina up to the doors of death. I am sharpening the point with two different arguments: that translating, our only legitimate way of querying whether un-translatability exists, by its nature precludes the discovery of what it seeks; and that translations and the originals they approximate coexist as mutually interflowing circuits of expression, approaching each other but never joining, leaning toward one another yet never quite symmetrically—since the original is privilegedly implicit to the points it wants to make. These two arguments derive from different perspectives—the first from that of the translator searching, and the second from that of an observer outside the translation work, who can see the pull of the Idea—what every original wants to be perfused by—as it draws translations up toward the force-zone of their original. Neither argument admits any absolute impediment to the achievement of translation, any factor of mere untranslatability; though both posit, as the ground for discovering this lack of impediment, endless work in the fields of quantity, *gradus*—slow *gradus*—*ad Parnassum*. Heine and Plato—my fragment was from the homoerotic grace of young Plato—belong to what we used to consider our *Kulturgebiet,* our culture-zone. What about translations from mind-zones farther from us in place or time or both? Has untranslatability a foothold there?

The Copper Eskimos—of Dolphin and Union Strait, Central Canadian Arctic—live their higher culture through dance-songs and incantations; group presentations to which individuals bring hope (for abundant seal harvests, for decent weather) and recent experience (a vast trek just completed, a hunt just observed). No experience is complete before it has been sung and danced in a public forum. These intricate, drum-accompanied seances strain our powers of understanding, force up from the TV set some gobot shaman enchanting the living room (see music score).[2] Translation? How is it possible? What will it have to take into consideration? Ciniciaq was a nonliterate Puivliq, deep in his *Gesamtkunstwerk* and miming a bear's mind. His F-major chant works through phrases of fairly regular measures, with cunningly varied numbers of beats. All that will have to be dealt with. And more. As translators we will have to deal with a refrain—e ye yi yai ye ye yi yai / ye yi yai ye ye yi yai—that repeats itself *after* the first and second (of the three) verses and then interweaves with the music of the third verse, which receives no refrain. Among other local conditions contributing to the virtually untranslatable, are frequent crowd interjections—*ho he ho he* cries. (The Copper Eskimos, excited at the first phonograph recordings of their songs in 1916, whooped it up in the background, as the cold wax testifies.) Inseparable from

this aural mélange, its natural heart, is the three-verse semantic nucleus:

> My child when it was about to cry,
> Four eyes though they followed us,
> Their little evacuation over there.

Runes, apothegms, even proverbs challenge our longing for meaning; force from us that on-the-line interest that drove Novalis (for instance) to the hieroglyph, to the holy carving; that drove Armand Schwerner to invent broken tablets; that holds us in the rain at Jurby Head staring at the inscriptions on Keltic crosses. But the anthropological conundrum embedded in dance-song threatens to down our longing. Isn't there too much hidden? What interpretative hope-step can we muster from the editor's gloss, "This was said to be the incantation of a polar bear that was pursued by a dog. The 'child' is the bear's cub, and the 'four eyes' are the dog's two eyes, and two white spots, one over each eye, which the bear mistook for another pair of eyes. The alternative reading for the last verse means 'we evacuated.' " From inside the bear, from inside her dance music, we must create our response.

> Furry zone of my gut ah pain ah pain ah pain
> Cub-dear ah pain ah pain ah pain
> Four eyes the Dog shadowed us ah pain ah pain
> Weeping from those eyes our wet dead urine ah pain ah pain ah pain

We must say it out, and over and through it must manage refrain and its variations, drum beat, and equivalents either of the large igloo or the tin-shed dance house. And while we are into our *style rétro* trip, we may as well project—outside and around us as rumor—the great war to be called *World War I*.

I near a saturation of my point. If any text threatens to be untranslatable, it will be the foregoing, a narrow bridge extended by collectors into the ice of an entirely oral tradition. All the translatable advantages Heine and Plato present from their stance inside us as a culture are lacking here. We are on our own. . . . The resultant hilarity, the *ivresse des grandes profondeurs,* all this thrills us here without guaranteeing us. What can we say for our defense of translatability in the present instance?

We are to some extent thrown back on the mere logic used above. Nothing outside our actual translation effort is qualified to disqualify our possibilities. As translators of this piece, we search from within and cannot be faulted from without. Or we present to the Copper Eskimo original a hemisphere of potential congruence, while we remain more than usually willing to withdraw and remake. But even in this case our self-defense is not abject or empty. We can at least evaluate—from the considerable in facts—the plausibility and energy of our translation response. We can learn more. We can read more. We can go to Fort Rupert. We can do a best that is not simply the best we can manage. Symptoms of that stripe are like "feeling well," which can, as we know, hide mortal illness but usually doesn't.

Finally a small poem so simple-perfect, so true in its own culture, that it helps us sustain every threat to the possibility of translation. And that from within undatable Manx, a twig, at least, of our own culture-tree:

C'raad t'ou goll?	Where are you going?
Goll dy schoill.	Going to school.
C'raad ta'n lioar?	Where is your book?
Ayns y drawer.	In the drawer.
C'raad ta'n drawer?	Where is the drawer?
Ayns y dresser.	In the dresser.
C'raad ta'n dresser?	Where is the dresser?
Ayns y thie.	In the house.
C'raad ta'n thie?	Where is the house?
Ayns y clieau.	In the mountain.
C'raad ta'n slieau?	Where is the mountain?
Ayns y voayl ve rieau.	Where it always was.[3]

(Translated by F. Will)

This time, one feels, there is only one way to translate— poorly but chainedly. The English words fall in place with that unreimagined clunk that will make them forever hard to revise. (Later and better versions will have to come from someone else.) And yet, the relative success of the translation is due to precisely that inevitable clunk, to that falling into place. The mystery of the final couplet is guaranteed to it by the original. *First Lessons in Manx*—a grammar and glossary—is all I needed.

Pound's daring as a translator, though known, has not yet subjected him to the inevitable fate of revolutionaries—indifference. A famed story puts Pound before a Li Po text in which there are crucial lacunae. Bearded Chinese scholars shake their heads at the loss and lament, expressing centuries of despair before the destructive accidents of history. Pound—leaning hard on Fennellosa—so penetratingly reads what remains of the Li Po text that he is able to suggest what has to have been there, what its integral form was. He fills the lacunae with himself, with his imagination. A few years later, thanks to the inevitable archaeologists, the missing manuscript is found and the lost lines are recovered. They are virtually as Pound reimagined them. The translator-historian has reentered a text on the farthest border from himself and made its meaning his. There is no need to add—to this description of intuitive success—that the translation Pound created from this foray was also a good poem.

In arguing against untranslatability earlier, I claimed no infinite powers for translation. I have not assumed translators like Ezra Pound. (My four example-barriers were hardly wiped away with a Poundian bravura.) Shelley, it is true, flew across time's barrier into the arms of Greek gold. Did he even, to some degree, brighten that gold? (Michel Leiris, translating Hopkins, is thought by many to have improved, deepened, his original; and Baudelaire may have done the same for Poe.) Heine—the closest example to us in time—remained almost untouched by our translation efforts. A Copper Eskimo dance-song excited me to imagine a *Gesamtkunstwerk*-response that would startle, reaching out self-consciously into an other that sends back no sound waves. And translating a Manx text, as I know myself, proved a conquest only because it was a conquest too easy. Fairly simple word placing met the demands of the original. The result was simple, perfect, and relatively uninteresting.

Infinite powers, no; Poundian powers, hardly; but powers there are—in my four translation examples and their varieties—

ample enough to show us countries beyond, implications of the translation act for other perspectives onto consciousness. I am thinking of some liminal issues I only brushed at the beginning: translating's relation to certain traits of the whole knowing process and, specifically, to traits of the process of knowing languages. I take up these twin points—language knowing and then knowing itself—separately.

First the act of knowing languages. What does the experience of translation help us to understand about that act? Translation includes no limits in its definition; I can translate from Hammurabi's code, the *Tao te ching*, or the *Njal's Saga*. This is no empty-freedom assertion, nor is it simply an assertion—though that is a good deal—that anything the human being can express in language can be meaningfully witnessed to, or testified to, in return. Saying that the definition of translation includes no limits means more, means that when we translate, we are recovering lost elements of ourselves. We are recuperating. How else could we manage to transcend time, space, and tone? How else than by an enacted realization that how we now say something is layered over other ways we are saying it or have said it? How—asked Goethe—could the eye see the sun were it not itself a sun? Implicit in this eternal-return realization is a sense of what is involved when we learn languages.

Have we to come to a theory of tongues? Humanity's descent into culture-history has meant a proliferation of linguistic, as of organic, species. Indo-European—Sanskrit—the Romance and Teutonic languages; that is sequence and specialization. Diversification dominates everywhere on this pattern. And we know where it all began:

> And they said: Come, let us make a city and a tower, the top whereof may reach to heaven: and let us make our name famous before we be scattered abroad into all lands.
>
> And the Lord came down to see the city and the tower, which the children of Adam were building.
>
> And he said: Behold, it is one people, and all have one tongue: and they have begun to do this, neither will they leave off from their designs, till they accomplish them in deed.
>
> Come ye, therefore, let us go down, and there confound their tongue, that they may not understand one another's speech.

> And so the Lord scattered them from that place into all lands, and they ceased to build the city.
>
> And therefore the name thereof was called Babel, because there the language of the whole earth was confounded; and from thence the Lord scattered them abroad upon the face of all countries.[4]

What better text to ground an account of translatability, to justify the hypothesis of fall from an original oneness? In the beginning, after all, was a Logos. What are we doing, in learning new languages, but recovering that Logos?

What about translation as model for the knowing process in general, the process that includes translation, learning languages, learning symbol systems? Knowing in general—like its subspecies, translating—always acts outward from itself; always culminates empty of validation and without guarantee. Translating well, like all outreaching knowing, feels good, feeds back into itself confirmingly, but must serve as its own authentication. The inherent gift from an effectual—I want to say authentic—translation is the will to translate more, a knowing that feels its known against it, that eventuates in an effective medicine or a steel-stress formula that enables bridges or a docu-poem the age sings in: knowing of those stripes makes more knowing of those stripes want itself. Translation and the knowing process it is embedded in are only and sufficient proofs of their own possibility, posit themselves continually—in the face of any proofs of their impossibility.

I am conscious here of a now Old Fashioned Existentialist tone, something weary playing around the edge of this self-impregnating discussion of the translation process—and now of the whole knowing and learning process. I hear the charge that the epistemology and aesthetic at work here are too anything-goes. And I hear laughter from that Theodor Adorno whose *Jargon of Authenticity* I translated ten years ago, finding as I worked how much I agree with him, how little I care for loose relativism or for the easy ascription of value to personal preferences. In response I look for a way to make clear both that translation (and knowing generally) travels open paths, walks loose in the galaxy; and that these acts are neither value-free nor exempt from self-bettering obligations.

Untermeyer, Draper, and Will all have a shot at Heine. Each worker from within his efforts went to what he constituted—in this instance—as an outer limit to his articulateness and imagination. Each had his version of what Heine was enabling him to say better than Heine. By standards inherent to each little piece of work—criteria like revision, direction changing, new-perception incorporation—each of these translators postulated standards of value in terms of which he was trying to adjust and modify and improve his own work. Those inherent standards—like the deductive principles or metaphorical dynamics available to any of us as knower—function from within the space-opening act of translation, to perfuse it with value. Nothing more than that is required, to guarantee to translation its lust for the good and to justify our search for the best in that good. Good translation, like any effectual knowing, is from within itself the discipline on which its absolute freedom depends.

Beauty As the Threshold
of Nature with Art

Pour l'inconscient de l'homme pétrisseur, l'ébauche est l'em-
bryon de l'oeuvre, l'argile est la mère du bronze.

Bachelard, *L'Eau et les rêves*

Beauty is that flash set off in matter when through its
knower it passes across a threshold, enters a new—
brighter and higher—condition. I stress the word
matter in this case because I'm emphasizing beauties either of art
(which organizes and expresses a material medium) or nature,
which is organized matter letting itself shine for us. I am not
thinking of the beauty of thought intersecting with thought or the
beauty of a love that has scraped itself as clean as possible—free of
the fish scales of time and place. I also stress a notion of the new
condition. I mean what Plotinus did in the *Enneads,* when he
claimed that the artist frees from nature intelligible beauty that was
only latent in it. This is the spiritualization of material.

Of interest to me is the point of crossing, and the maieutic
that draws matter up into its fullest expression. I have long been
looking for mind-allies in the mapping of this topography—which
was the work of my first published thought-prose, *Intelligible
Beauty in Aesthetic Thought* (1958).[1] There I surveyed the tradition
of matter-made-into-beauty as it made a history of itself from the
thought of Plato to that of Victor Cousin. The growth-points—
from which I felt my argument take energy of itself—were in
Plotinus, Winckelmann, Goethe and Herder, thought-feeling clus-

ters from which grew the widening perception that the beautiful
is an aspect of the true and at least a spur to the good. I was looking
for the thresholds in those feelers' thought, where the beautiful is
thrust up into perception.

In another book, *Literature Inside Out*,[2] I discovered a contemporary thinker, Adrian Stokes, in whom I found unusual support
toward the threshold aesthetic I was establishing. The Stokes work
in question was *Greek Culture and the Ego* (1958), which seemed
to me to penetrate some (supposed) mysteries of classical Hellen-
ism and to do so through a view of the transformation of nature.
Working from Melanie Klein's analyses of early childhood, Stokes
put great stress on the importance of the integrated ego and the
tamed superego in the formation of the Greek plastic and literary
achievement. That integration provided the finest Greek artists—
and many fifth-century Athenians to boot—with an acquisitive
and clear-sighted view of the object world, of which they could,
without in the process being enveloped, construct clear and copious
images. The happiness of this I-other conjunction was decisive for
the Greek achievement and underlay the Hellenic discovery of the
mind—of mind as philosophical inquiry, as aesthetic shaping, as
moral self-scrutinizer. (It may also have underlain the discovery of
all those thing- and concept-names in their distinctness, which have
made of Greek the ground-base of our Western vocabulary.) The
integration at work here, penetrating a society with itself, was in
various senses work with nature. The natural materials of art—
limestone, parchment, pigment-giving rocks—were finding their
whole object-condition, raised as they were by the integrated ego's
imagination. At the same time, the ego of the creator, in making
itself the transforming force, was becoming—with the art it created—a self-spiritualizing nature. In the art work—the pieces of
sculpture, the temple, the clay—the maker's and the medium's
natural dimension is surpassed and clarified. All this Stokes ar-
ranged to say with compact clarity in *Greek Culture and the Ego*
and, doing so, strengthened the fabric of the Plotinian tradition's
efforts to enrich nature by its higher forms.

Years later I see the larger uses of Stokes' work to anyone
concerned with the nature-beauty threshold. I have in mind a small
anthology of works that swarm over my earlier perceptions: works

by Carl Sauer (especially *Land and Life*), J. Frank Dobie (*The Mustangs*), Roy Bedichek (*Adventures with a Texas Naturalist*), Louis Mumford *(The City in History)*, Fustel de Coulanges *(La Cité antique)*, Vincent Scully *(The Earth, The Temple, and the Gods)*, Charles Olson *(Bibliography of America for Ed Dorn)*. I see that naturalism and the work of the naturalists flows continuously into the work and thought of culture—into art. I find new texts on the shelf, and last of all Stokes' earlier work, *The Stones of Rimini* (1934), and his later essence-scratchers like *Rough and Smooth*. In them, though less directly put than in *Greek Culture,* lie formulations of astounding vigor anent the power of nature to propose its ascents and that of mind—the appropriative mind—to accept that proposal.

Stokes writes, in *The Stones of Rimini,* about the Tempio Malatesta commissioned and ordered in the mid–fifteenth century by Duke Sigismondo in Rimini; and about the exemplary carver-architect, Agostino, who carried out the commission. But the theme of Stokes' presentation (and his deepest passion) is simply the Mediterranean world—its physical-spiritual properties and its effects on people born there. One might almost say that his main theme is limestone and the material fantasies awakened in Silurian-based man—as he is drawn by his water-stone culture backward into the primary memories he is.

First, to take Stokes in characteristic pose: "For instance, at one point at least where horizontal strata are exposed on the cliffs at Lavenock, Glamorgan, one sees the delicate lines as architrave moulding and a projecting slab above as cornice."[3] The perception is typical for the Stokes of this book. With ease he resurrects elements of the perspective specifically dear to Plotinus. (Stokes eschews system as such but cuts into the Plotinian view at many places.) Plotinus cognizes what is as a vast coherent system, a monism, in which all is ordered by its level of reality—and in which each inferior level longs (strives, presses) for the level just above it. (All depends from its source, the emanating good, and longs up-ward half-articulately toward that source.) The sculptor is the ar-chetypal eliciter. By characteristic act he or she breaks curiously into the granite slab, seeking. (That *curiously* is a key term only abstractly explored by Plotinus; and in it lies much of the threshold *mysterium* this book is about. Stokes will give us some hints on the sculptor's motive. The testifying I mentioned anent the translation motive, and the aesthetic "curiosity" I am onto now as a motive for carving have in common that they both spring loose a new zone of production, cross into fresh perception.) Carving inward, the sculptor finds the generative lines in the stone—its desire lines—and cleaves the stone along them. The stone opens to him, letting him find inside it the face or form it wishes to let him make of it. That letting and willing will be first of all the stone's, though the form its resultant assumes will depend on whether the quarrier is Giacometti, Meštrović, or Rodin. Something of that stone-and-nature will concerns Stokes too, later and in the passage cited above.

Nature at its most expressive contains, for Stokes, an invitation to the artist (an invitation—which, as in the Plotinian account, stems from the stone or mountain's self-interest—to rise). In the Mediterranean basin this invitation is at its most articulate, because there the symbiosis of water with limestone has generated a carvable medium that engages with our deepest visual imagination. The engagement is guaranteed by the pull, on us, of a matter-medium that embodies, or is, the zone of many of our deepest fantasies. The Istrian limestone (for example) is crowded with marine fossils of the Cretaceous Age, chunks of reminder of our prehistoric origins in the sea. We are drawn back into that chunky materiality, coaxed to stroke—as we are, claims Stokes, by the smooth-rough marble of balustrade, door knocker, and windowsill wherever in Italy the Quattrocento has left its mark. The pull is deeper, too—and takes us closer yet to that threshold mystery. We are literally revoked by the Mediterranean limestone to our primal consciousness—a sure-making source: "Limestone, for the most part formed of organic deposits, is the link between the organic and inorganic worlds. Limestone exhibits in mummified state the life no longer found of this Silurian and other distant ages."[4] That link, which we contain in ourselves but long to free to our sight and understanding, is activated by the watery dimension: "In all stonework typically Mediterranean there is somewhere expressed the identification or mutual consummation of limestone and water, there is expressed water made solid, permanent, glowing instead of glassy, yet in space and brightened by the dripping rains."[5] How does Stokes account for our response to these primal zones that lie both inside us and in the stone?

Carving and moulding are the two dominant sculptural procedures. Carving is cutting into the stone so as to release its life in its own voice; and, as such, carving of limestone or marble remains a rare but effectual conduit for nature's voice. (Stokes laments the passing of carving—which in the West has been the particular genius of the Greeks and the Quattrocento but which in Stokes' Britain—of the second quarter of this century—could be seen yielding to every version of the modern jerry-built—in private housing, public buildings, handicrafts; and on a higher level to plastic treatment of material wherever the arts express themselves.) Carving as such—and especially as we see it on the Tempio Malatesta, in Agostino's work—is a true wooing of the limestone, a male act with a woman, an entering, eliciting; and then a begetting of progeny—the forms the sculpture turns up. "As for representation of the human form, it will readily be understood that in the carving of stone's hard luminous substance, it suffers all the stroking and polishing, all the definition that our hands and mouths bestow on those we love."[6] Here we have our sculptural motif developed in Stokesian terms, a motif he will extend in *Greek Culture and the Ego,* turning out a Freudian account of the sense-harmony we long to establish with nature as material. (Something neo-Kantian clings to this account of new nature-harmonies, though for Stokes there is no doubt that the aesthetic imagination can penetrate nature as it is.) The motif appears more sharply when to it we contrast that relatively conceptual work (sculptural or architectural) for which the Germans (as Stokes puts it) have the horrid word *Plastik* (Stokes calls this work *modelling* or *moulding*): "One can say at once of modelling forms (as opposed to carving forms) in the widest sense, that they are without restraint: I mean that they can well be the perfect *embodiment* of conception: whereas, in the process of carving, conception is all the time adjusted to the life that the sculptor feels beneath his tool."[7] Modelling, we assume, is almost without restraint the mode of our day. Rodin and Le Corbusier are named as higher examples of it, but

Stokes deprecated his age in which "synthetic materials take the place of age-old products in which fantasy is deposited." It can hardly surprise us that these perspectives, which Stokes was forming in Italy from 1926 to 1928, brought him together there—and precisely in terms of the Rimini temple—with Ezra Pound. The two men's views interwove at that time.

Do other arts than sculpture and architecture—originally arts of stone, and Stokes' prime examples—pass upward through their media, cross thresholds into our consciousness? Or has Stokes built only the fragments of an aesthetic out of a unique group of arts?

Let's take the hardest cases, literature and music. Are their resultant arts in any sense carved (released, unbound) out of a medium into an expression that is the progeny of artist mating with the outer world? Or are the media of such arts radically separate from the medium of sculpture?

Language is the medium of literature. Words in their orders and planned disorders constitute the stuff of literature. *Langue* and *parole* equally, and in mutual intersections, undergird verbal art. But this medium presents two constitutive differences from the medium of sculpture. Language, from which the writer will create his artifact, is material in a different sense from limestone—whose kickable opposition to us is part of its drawing power. I am not suggesting that language is not material. But I am suggesting— and this is difference number two—that because language is to some extent the tool with which the writer raids language, therefore language's materiality as medium is compromised. At the very least we need to abandon—when we talk of literature—the sculptural model of imagining mind here, eliciting medium there. Given *this* difference however—and much more can be said of it in its place— I see no reason to exclude literature from the aesthetic Stokes is establishing. Language is plundered by imagination working through *parole;* or, turned to another light, the expressive needs of a *langue* can be felt pressing outward toward expression—are, as some have said, the continual longings of a people's voice to be what it can be for self-reflection.

Music? Can we extend a Stokes-Plotinus perspective to the negotiation that generates music? Once again the problem of materiality needs restatement. *Langue* and *parole* exist here too. *Langue* will be the history of musical possibilities and impossibilities, as it presents itself to the composer in his or her moment, while *parole* will be his or her individual idiom. Musical tradition will solicit enrichments and bringings-up-to-date of itself, in just the way the tribe's language will (though here lies a discrepancy between language, which is not artistically preformed and an age's music, which *is* preformed: raw sound—the closer equivalent to *langue*—simply cannot serve as the medium of musical composition). With some careful distinction, our discussion of the genesis of music will follow that of literature into a broadly Stokesian perspective.

Now for a contrast. Stokes himself occupies an unmodish worldview. His nature-romanticism, his old-style aestheticism, his alliance to the Platonic position: all this places him nowhere or in an antiwhere of his century and time (not to mention our time, which will barely extend an antenna in such a tradition's direction). In an opposite nowhere vibrates the work of a scientist-psychologist like John Watson, whose *Behaviorism* (published in 1924, four years before *The Stones of Rimini*) illustrates how brashly anti-Stokesian a Stokes contemporary could be. Watson's interest in the "aesthetic" is nugatory, yet the few points he makes are strong—radiantly clear and simpleminded. They can and will introduce a variety of aesthetic views that spring from hostility either to the Plotinian-Stokesian axis or even to a humane historicism.

Watson considered thinking talking to oneself and, conversely, viewed language (voiced or unvoiced) to be the total coin of the mind's work. For him there was no mystery either to language or to thought. No depth either.

His Enlightenment contempt for mystery extends directly to the mystery of the aesthetic, which he takes glee in puncturing. Art in words, he seems ready to concede, is thought to spring from the new, the unhackneyed—from that which is not the direct provocation of a stimulus—as Watson normally assumes effects to be. But then how does this new come into existence? (Is it—I ask—from some mating of creative imagination with nature, matter, in the air of material fancy?) "The answer is that we get them (new verbal creations such as a poem or a brilliant essay) by manipulating words, shifting them about until a new pattern is hit upon." But then why can some people master such manipulating and others not? It is because the literary creator "has manipulated words under the influence of emotional and practical situations of one kind or another, as we have manipulated the keys of the typewriter or a group of statistics, or wood, brass and lead." No particular organ is attributed to the artist, only practice in the domain he or she happened to choose. Why though, we still ask, does the artist innovate in language? Why does he or she "manipulate" or "shift" words around? Watson moves toward an answer by reference to Patou's gown making. Patou—Watson guesses—throws some fabric over a model, then works with it, tries it out this way and that, until at last he discovers that he has made a new creation. He cries "Voilá, parfait," without realizing what he has been working toward. Artworks come about that randomly, Watson claims. (But even granted that Patou is an artist, the question remains, What leads him into the creative fiddling? Watson builds no context of explanation. He is far too anxious to depreciate the origins of art, though in the Patou case he stumbles on fertile explanations, which would not at all detract from the *mysterium artis*.)

One additional passage, and I deal with it out of fairness to Watson's challenge:

> The painter plies his trade in the same way, nor can the poet boast of any other method. Perhaps the latter has just read Keats, perhaps he is just back from a moonlight walk in the garden, perchance his beautiful fiancée has hinted just a little strongly that he has never sung her charms in sufficiently impassioned phrases. He goes to his room, the situation is set for him, the only way he can escape it is to do something and the only thing he can do is to manipulate words. The touch of the pencil starts the verbal activity just as the whistle of the referee at the football games releases a group of fighting, struggling men. Naturally words expressive of the romantic situation he is in soon flow—being in that situation he could not compose a funeral dirge nor a humorous poem. Again the situation he is in is slightly different from any other he was ever in before and therefore the pattern of his word creation will also be slightly new.[8]

Here Watson bows toward the motive problem, tries to make us see creative fiddling as both random—because without depth, surface skittering—and motivated, provoked by a (perfectly banal) desire to please. In his bow Watson goes further than before toward making the aesthetic motive convincing, and the endurance of art seem more than an accident. But in bowing he expounds with fresh blatancy the pathetic shallowness he wills into his position. (A shallowness, of course, that Watson believed in—intelligently— and thought publically useful to recognize as part of the description of homo sapiens.) His protagonists are of cardboard, their inter- action lifeless; and no attention is given to the existential motives— like fear of loss, or holding the present—that even foes of the poetic usually concede to be part of it.

Watson may be a straw man for me, in the sense that his argument is syncopated and dismissive, but the values he developed in *Behaviorism* attack human potency at a point assaulted by many today. (*Le beau, le vrai, le bien:* Who of intelligence today upholds any such values, without complicated shading and defensive pro- legomena?) These many include the hordes of latter-day behavior- ists, dinky technocrats of the soul; but also the priests of disorder (or new order or unorder, a variety of guises)—Cage, Heisenberg, Beckett, Bridgman, Prigogine, Lacan, Derrida. These latter man- darins, far from the locked universe of dated behaviorism, far closer to the chance order of Lucretius, join the Watsonians in one simple conviction-block: that the great chain of being is broken, that man is no soul-ful intelligencer and recreator of the whole, that beauty, in conjunction perhaps with truth and goodness, is either an out- dated or a downright inapropos concept. The nature-beauty threshold with what it connotes has no place in this world picture. The perspective from which I opened this book—that untranslat ability is meaningless—itself rests inside assumptions that neither Watson nor Cage would accept; especially the assumption of a continuous universe that progressively unfolds itself as meaning— to us as frontier discoverers.

The tradition Plotinus and Stokes occupy—and which accom- modates the translation perspectives of my first essay—expressed itself to perfection in certain eighteenth-century Germans.

Let us imagine the great chain of being intact, its links transitions and gleaming thresholds. This structure of order and transition is a frame for the experience of beauty as threshold. Winckelmann characteristically places himself at the maieutic crossing between nature and its overlink, culture, characteristically sees beauty as a product of such transition: "Der Begriff der Schönheit ist wie ein aus der Materie durchs Feuer gezogener Geist."[9] "Spirit of matter," an essence, expresses to perfection that inside-out self-transcendence that the artist enables nature to perform of itself. (Stokes could hardly have turned the figure with more cunning interiority.) It's worth restating, in this view, the Plotinus tradition's insistence that the beautiful is identical with a transformation in nature. Never has it been better said than by Winckelmann that the transformation is a sucking up, upward (chain of being, epistrophe-conduit, breath being sucked back to its source: so many images for the longing in the great return).

Goethe writes into Winckelmann's traces and exceeds him in the discoveries his aesthetic humanism permits. Art does not imitate nature but must learn how nature does its works: "Wir zuletzt beim Kunstgebrauch nur dann mit der Natur wetteifern können, wenn wir die Art, die sie bei Bildung ihrer Werke verfährt, ihr wenigstens einigermassen abgelernt haben"[10] (Goethe, this, who discovered the maxillary bone by inferring what nature, jaw constructing as it does, must have included in the mouth—though the bone structure traces could at that time only be hypothesized). Bringing nature's work-methods into our art, we crack open the boundary between nature and ourselves: "Umgeben von antiken Statuen empfindet man sich in einem bewegten Naturleben."[11] Nature's life—where it is most effectively organized—is released by ancient statuary into Nature's presence to us. (What Goethe found in the classical *Statuenkabinett* I find in the forest of Henry Moore sculptures in the Royal Ontario Museum, Toronto.) Two more passages should do to hold this Goethean point and leave it for a benchmark in the vast sea between Plotinus and Stokes: "Zum Schönen wird erfordert ein Gesetz, das in die Erscheinung tritt.— Beispiel von der Rose. In den Blüten tritt das vegetabilische Gesetz in seine höchste Erscheinung, und die Rose wäre nur wieder der Gipfel dieser Erscheinung."[12] What argument could more effectively go to the heart of this essay? Beauty here is integral to the way the universe is put together. Humanist because naturalist, Goethe will in the final analysis welcome the return by which man, opening nature's beauty into itself, finds himself. A distinctive ontology justifies artist man's effort to open nature onto himself as beauty: "Der letzte Produkt der sich immer steigernden Natur ist der schöne Mensch."[13]

Aesthetic threshold thoughts. I enlarge the chrestomathy into our century. Two more thinkers: Gabriel Marcel and Jacques Maritain.

Rilke gave the impetus to Marcel's most extensive criticism: two Paris lectures given in 1944.[14] The tone—in World War crisis—is of infinite respect for one who believed in the sacredness of life as well as in the creative interpenetration of death and life.

From the outset Marcel values Rilke's testifying—to the ancient and rich presence of life. "It is of the essence of Rilke's vision, or again of the power of vibration at the heart of his work, not to isolate the artist from creation in general." Whether as center of creation or as witness to it, the artist is there for all enduring and genesis. (This sounds like the testifying of which I earlier found the translator's act an instance. The translator goes to the code, presents himself as his version of it, and truly—like Patou—says, *Voilá, I have valued and praised this work; I testify to it!*) Rilke's, like Plotinus', artist occupies a position at the center of the cosmos.

From that position, Marcel thinks, Rilke's artist knows how much death there is in circumambient life, and how much life there is in that death. This death is in part a question of lack (or defect), which forever wishes supplementing: "The great death which each man bears within himself is the fruit around which everything gravitates." (This lack is that Plotinian deprivation felt by the uplonging strata of emanation, or Stokes' cry from the Silurian, whose watery fossil beds lure us back.) Like the Plotinian artist, Rilke's— and Marcel's—poet must patiently stand close to the longing and deprived things of his world. (Things here are *Dinge* not *Sache*; nature-immersed things, not the humanized.) Patience of that stamp, the Plotinian mark, Rilke learned from Rodin (Marcel guides the argument in among his favorites, includes Nerval):

"What he contemplates exists for him to the exclusion of all the rest, it is the world where everything is happening; when he carves out a hand this hand is alone in space, there is nothing else." Plotinus and Stokes (and Goethe and Kazantzakis) have to be audible here, voicing. Rodin's hand is for each of them the human-seeking embrace from the mineral bed.

Marcel dwells on Rilke's Ninth Duino Elegy, in which the human mission to live and hold the transitory is most intensely expressed. Rilke had often felt on him the pressure and demand of the animal world—which for him existed more purely and more nearly originally than mankind itself. Animals—and on one occasion a battalion of lizards—could easily obsess him, make him testify to their presence. That incumbency would be the hard start of art: "To recreate a thing, that meant having been everywhere, having kept nothing back, left nothing out, betrayed nothing; it meant knowing the hundreds of profiles. . . ." In the Ninth Elegy that hard start is demanded:

> Earth, is it not just this that you want: to arise
> invisibly in us? Is not your dream
> to be one day invisible? Earth! Invisible!
> What is your urgent command, if not transformation?
> Earth, you darling, I will! Oh, believe me, you need
> no more of your spring-times to win me over; a single one,
> ah one, is already more than my blood can endure.
> Beyond all names I am yours, and have been for ages.[15]

Marcel adds, interacting with Rilke's argument, "Are we perhaps in the world in order to utter the primitive words which clothe earthly experience with a body: house, bridge, water-spring, orchard, window and again pillar or tower, but also to translate that intimate inward being of which things in themselves are unconscious?"

Here we halt, and think. Marcel (and Rilke, his voice here) widens the Plotinian frame, perhaps in places stretches it out of shape. (Stokes and Goethe had already punched—or, should we say, accented—it; but less than will Marcel, less still than Maritain.) Plotinus himself was a systematizer, mystic, or philosopher as you prefer, who understood the *Weltall* precisely as a multilayered epistrophe. Animal or plant life, as it rose into the sculptor's purposes, carried out a general law of spiritualization demonstrable throughout creation. In *The Stones of Rimini* Stokes laid his emphasis on three themes that remind us of Plotinus' pertinence: the deep grounding of man in his natural frame; the mutual love (or eros) that draws the natural strata up to man, man down into them and up; and the inclusion of art, which elevates, in the very work of the cosmos making itself. Goethe still works this conceptual territory, himself responsible as natural historian, genius of making, mythicist not quite cut from the old dispensations, the chain of being glistening in his hands. We have seen that he—say, in the Law of the Rose passage—rigorously inserts the human act into the self-enrichment of nature. Thresholds to cross, being-zones to undertake: such landscaping appears in the last degree congenial to Goethe.

Marcel (Rilke) generalizes out from the armature of the Plotinian. What strikes me, however, is the flexibility of that armature. The required assumptions are evident: that the aesthetic springs from the constitution of things; that man's own fulfillment is connected with releasing the beauty from nature (or from himself as nature); and that the good of things in general is enhanced by the art-making procedure. Marcel (and Rilke) constantly turn up this perspective. Rilke, particularly, hears the call of the purely natural as it longs to be testified to and then, in that audition, understands how fine it is to be here, "because being here amounts to so much, because all this Here and Now so fleeting seems to require us and strangely concerns us."[16]

That *seems to require,* with its confident immensity, places us deep in the *Weltall.*

Maritain, like Marcel, speaks from deep in the Catholicism of mid-twentieth-century France, though with a Thomistic integrity that could hardly be farther—inside a single thought-family—from Marcel's sympathy for *Existenz,* for the concrete in the flux of time.

Like Rilke, Maritain places the poet, the artist in the widest sense, close to that nature with which he is consubstantial, in and through which he creates. Try reading the whole from a single passage, in the vast *Creative Intuition in Art and Poetry:*

> Poetic intuition is directed toward concrete existence as connatural to the soul pierced by a given emotion: that is to say, each time toward some

singular existent, toward some complex of concrete and individual reality, seized in the violence of its sudden self-assertion and in the total unicity of its passage in time. This transient motion of a beloved hand—it exists an instant, and will disappear forever, and only in the memory of angels will it be preserved, above time. Poetic intuition catches it in passing, in faint attempt to immortalize it in time. But poetic intuition does not stop at this given existent, it goes beyond, and infinitely beyond. Precisely because it has no conceptualized object, it tends and extends to the infinite, it tends toward all the reality, the infinite reality which is engaged in any singular existing thing, either the secret properties of being involved in its identity and in its existential relations with other things, or the other realities, all the other aspects or fructifications of being, scattered in the entire world, which have in themselves the wherewithal to found some ideal relation with this singular existing thing, and which it conveys to the mind, by the very fact that it is grasped through its union with, and resonance in subjectivity spiritually awakened.[17]

Once more the poet—as representative art maker—has his being close to the things of the world. (*Things:* how important they become in this thought-domain, from Plotinus to Rilke, to Maritain's "singular existent . . . seized in the violence of its sudden self-assertion and . . . its passage in time.") Once more the poet stands close to the presence of things—as did Rodin, as does the ideal god-shaping poet in Heidegger's "Vom Ursprung des Kunstwerkes." The work of the poet toward the attended-to object— hands again, Rilke-Rodin hands—seems at first an effort to stop the flux of time, one more ploy in the ancient *ô temps suspends ton vol* maneuver. But Maritain goes at once to a more substantive account of the artist's work—to work taking place in the "open zone" around things: "Poetic intuition does not stop at the given existent; it goes beyond, and infinitely beyond." Poetry—unlike, say, painting—has no object (landscape, building-scape) but works out into existence through the infinite network of *realia,* that concrete existence the imaginative work itself expresses. (Maritain's sentence on network syntactically mimes the intricate and closed world it is describing and reminds us how fully he insists on his place in the kind of spiritual monism I am reviewing here.) In one of his remarks on fiction—in the vulgar sense—Maritain indicates the mission of the novelist: "Only an exceptionally powerful poetic intuition can cause the relationship between the novelist and his characters to be what it must be—an image, I mean, of the relationship between the transcendent creative eternity of God and the free creatures who are both acting in liberty and firmly embraced by His purpose."[18] High transformation of the empirical, the novelist's mission; Maritain once again convinced that the artist transmutes the daily in order to offer to the high ones. Plotinus, Rilke, and Stokes all come by such thought onto a belief in angels.

One more line of Maritain, taking us to the farthest border of the Plotinian and inviting in the aleatory counter. I think of "The more the poet grows, the deeper the level of creative intuition descends into the density of his soul." What could mark this tradition more strongly than its assumption of the reality of depth? What tradition could make it more feasible to define depth? That definition: depth is the created world's accessible insistence, at every level of its self-expression, on the presence in it of multiple layers, of zones of interiority that can be attained only by penetration but that await and even solicit that finding.

Aleatory music, chance-imagery poetry, indeterminacy physics: what symptoms are more resonant than these, of the twentieth-century assault on the universe-encased, nature-transforming work of beauty, the artwork in classic Western dress?

John Cage (in *Silence*) and George Brecht (in a potent essay on chance imagery)[19] argue chance into the heart of aesthetic integrity and in so doing—while asserting certain old continuities of art with nature—under-wound the Plotinian vision. For Cage "there is no such thing as an empty space or an empty time," and in fact we are unable even to create silence. The ever-presence of sound is infinitely diverse in its presence to us, and as artists we only now begin to cope with that infinity. (Multiple tapes, special amplifiers, prepared pianos: all aid us in making ourselves receptacles of diversity, affirmers of the richness of audible life—which Cage wishes us to be.) Ranging more widely, opening ourselves in music-testimony to the whole of sound, we become far more complete artists than were the maestros of the tradition. The resultant artworks are a living interrogation of the classical artwork's assumptions.

Cage's challenge to the Plotinian aesthetic, with its edifying thresholds, is the stronger for including in itself a telos—the awakening of life affirmation—and for embracing its own relation to nature. (Cage feels certain that the deep artist-nature relation is a thinning and narrowing of the artist's ability to testify.) What we can reply to Cage will be clearer when we add to his argument strands from Brecht and Heisenberg. But for the moment, this: Cage's break against traditional sound organization, against the history of the growth of the musician's material, radically ignores the change medium-history works in the materials available to the artist. The history of any given art becomes that art—changes the reality-continuum accordingly—and cannot be dismissed. Thresholds—such as that we posit here between nature and art, over the line into beauty—mark out perennial topography that cannot be erased by a confusion of nature with art.

George Brecht's essay on chance imagery praises the random, the aleatory, for its purging of the artist's creation—stripping it of the narrowly personal and opening it to nature. Once again then— and here in an essay testing various methods for attaining the purely random in art—the stress is on the superiority of a chance perspective. "As art approaches chance-imagery"—says Brecht—"the artist enters a oneness with all of nature." The challenge is acute. Brecht implies that the art tradition narrows the exposure of the artist to nature—to the impinging and available world that constitutes his material. We understand this better, momently: "Chance in the arts provides a means for escaping the biases engrained in our personality by our culture and personal past history, that is, it is a means of attaining greater generality." We are not, he argues, simply increasing our exposure to the vital, but we are breaking from the bonds of our past. Once more I may want to consider, from the Plotinian standpoint, what we remain determined to retain. Perhaps we should settle for a restatement of the function and context of the artist. Maritain, working genially from within that tradition, describes the intuitive intelligence with which the artist puts his material at his disposal. Chance-openness is not needed to provoke or safeguard the artist's independence or penetration; for the artist, by the freshness of his position in the forever forming "open" around things, cannot fail to explore their ever new meaning to him. Marcel's Rilke establishes an even more world-sensitive artist figure, than whom one can scarcely imagine a more open or general sensibility, one freer of any mere encumbrance from its tradition.

We near Heisenberg and that deepest of all assaults—the principle of indeterminacy—on the essentially ordered world structure presupposed by our Plotinians. I shear off a pair of observations as they pertain. Noting that we are "not only spectators but are always participants on the stage of life"[20] and that now the physicist gets "not a picture of nature" but a "picture of our relation to nature," Heisenberg restates his breathtaking convictions: that our measuring equipment obscures the physical objects we are measuring so that we can never acquire a stable-objective view of the fundamental physical world; and that such limitations force us to see the indeterminable behavior of material particles. Brecht's and Cage's arguments—as we sampled them—clearly run at their ease beside Heisenberg's technical witness.

Heisenberg points hesitantly to the arts and culture of his moment and risks thinking that an embracing condition—more copious than individual developments of matter or mind—establishes the awareness available to that moment. His own time—1958 and immediately before—seemed to him anguishingly transitional. What lay ahead of the indeterminate world picture? Was there a new-order vision in store, for which the culture-indeterminacy of the day would later seem to have been rich preparation? Within the principle of indeterminacy, Heisenberg appears to say, lies the conviction that it is itself not a final condition; not that it promises to yield to a new determinacy, a new Newtonianism—for such was not Heisenberg's position—but that it has within it no grounds for assuming its own finality.

Derrida, Foucault, and Sontag: a mixed society of non-Plotinians who, in essays written in the late sixties—ten years later than the triad discussed above—carve up text and author, work and maker, damage integrity with the verve of gene splicers.

I think of Susan Sontag's glistening "Aesthetics of Silence" (1967),[21] which dissects the antiart aesthetic of her day. That moment seems one in which, as Beckett put it, "there is nothing to express . . . together with the obligation to express." Artists of magnitude—Rimbaud, Wittgenstein, Duchamp—have in the recent past honored art by deserting it. They have refused all art heroics, all *poète maudit* self-aggrandizings, for a kind of *askesis,* a self-denial in which the highest art is intentionally impoverished—like a Jasper Johns canvas. Sontag insists that a new kind of silence is introduced with this *via negativa* work. The difference between Rilkean silence and that of Cage will help us understand her point. Rilke's silence in the Ninth Duino Elegy is a brooding patience over the mute but longing, humble things of the world (those natural objects whose latent meaning the Plotinian artist intuits and cooperates with). A benign nominalist, Rilke retains his faith in the saving power of language. Cage, on the other hand, believes in the antiart of opening the ears—to all available sounds; believes in the silence of an undifferentiated plenum. Though he calls this attending an "affirmation of life," he denies in it "the traditional hierarchies of interest and meaning, in which some things have more 'significance' than others." He turns his attention—as Sontag admiringly notes—to the simple happening. Her preferred solution to the art dilemma accumulating here, is Novalis': "Speaking for the sake of speaking is the formula of deliverance." Beckett, quite naturally, is her model for this self-saving.

What Heisenberg, Brecht, and Cage start to sense—that the artist-medium-artwork interaction must now be radically reformulated—is in Sontag brought to full expression. The artist is a kind of moment's saint practicing against his medium, even against his skill, to testify—to give voice to a time of dearth. Now, however, the dearth is not that pregnant waiting for the *kommende Götter,* which Heidegger saluted in "Vom Ursprung des Kunstwerkes," but is truly a dry cough, dry heave, whose power only its honesty guarantees. Threshold crossing is not irrelevant here. There is a new organization of interiorized nature, a new form made. But the actualizing artist is no longer a central eliciter, nor are his stuff or his product disclosures of a stable universe.

I pick from Derrida and Foucault essays that decapitate art structure and author identity; simplifying their complex, though inflated, arguments and heading for the old point—that the anti-

Plotinian perspective is here far into its radicalism, with a total subversion of the older thresholding frame. Derrida—in "Structure, Sign, and Play"[22]—attacks the "concept of centered structure," which is "a play constituted on the basis of a fundamental immobility and a reassuring certitude, which itself is beyond the reach of play." This reassuring certitude—which structuralism reinforced—is for Derrida another corollary of the persistent metaphysic of Being, which has questioned itself in his time. Lévi-Strauss is taken as the model of this questioning—in his laying down of a structuralist perspective, then intruding into and through it as *bricoleur*. (For Derrida the bricolage move is emblematic of the event by which a metaphysic of presence is brought into question.) Such bricolage was Lévi-Strauss' way of discovering the "non-essential structures of inherited thought," their shifting and play. The case of myth analysis becomes typically revealing, for there Lévi-Strauss discovers that there is no unity or absolute source of myth. The forms or the source of any myth are always shadows and virtualities, elusive, unactualizable, and nonexistent. (Lévi-Strauss goes on to observe that his own book about myths is a kind of myth.) Reading texts—myths, art works—is always part of a supplementarity: the moment of play, permitted by the lack or absence of a center or origin, is the movement of supplementarity—of our addition (as readers) of a new center and accordingly a new frame. Such playful addition is in constant tension against a metaphysic of Presence and is the active sign of our deconstructing the text by reading it. On this account thresholds are forever newly found when texts become a new form of supplement.

The instability of the text from within provokes its own continued self-confirmation. Whenever such an infinite—but untotalizable—being-structure deploys itself, we will have thresholds aplenty, thresholds virtually identical with the element of change. But I argue for the superior threshold, for those border crossings at which the artwork hovers—ready to become nature transformed, ready to testify to man the new-through-his-deed, ready to give teleologically into the whole. Thresholds of that substantiality, as they are called into being by the master translator or master sculptor, belong to a meaning-whole whose integrity reinforces every act internal to it. Derrida's assault—though of course this may be

no argument against its validity—turns very little back into itself;
converts itself—quite willedly of course—into no new richness of
perspective. With Derrida, who is working in the climate Sontag
analyzed, the category of richness—like that of depth—goes out
the window.

Foucault observes—in his essay "What Is an Author?"[23]—
that Derrida is far too conservative in his critique of orthodox
aesthetic categories. The signifier-signified axis, for instance, still
backbones Derrida's thought, assuring it of its old ties, its rooting
in the concept of a (classical) namer and named, creator and created,
origin and genesis. Foucault's own essay—he thinks—takes off
from a current perception that is far more penetrating than Derrida's assumptions: from a new indifference to "who said or wrote
it," to *authorship*.

Writing, now, with its emphasis on the sign as a game, "is a
question of creating a space into which the writing subject constantly disappears." The gamelike weeds of the writing act—its
close alliance with a coming supplement—assure it a spacious
insubstantiality; and in that project the author disappears—into
one of the author functions assigned to him as part of the discourse
of his age. The author's name, for instance, functions as do other
proper nouns: "The name of the author seems always to be present,
marking off the edges of the text, revealing, or at least character-
izing, its mode of being." In this elementary name-function, the
author is given by grammar the extension of his work. From this
simple point, passing through historical exempla, Foucault points
out how society has established the author—the literary author
since the seventeenth century—as a guarantor of the identity of
groups of works, as a voice responsible for its propositions, in short
as a "variable and complex function of discourse," "whose broadest
function is to aid in limiting the too-wide plenum of meanings" (I
leave out the connecting tissue here). The author becomes the
"principle of thrift in the proliferation of meanings." Put another
way, perhaps more plainly, the author is the means "by which one
impedes the free circulation, the free manipulation, the free composition, decomposition, and recomposition of fiction." The author, far from being an originary genius, or for that matter even
Watson's palper, is a fiction society speaks for its own advantage.

Foucault's developing concern with power hovers around this essay. But the point for us is clear: that Foucault is inverting the author's power in the author-work-medium relation. We have already seen text or work, as well as medium or means, torn from a monistic perspective, left flapping in contemporary shreds. Now we have the author dismembered—not in the older-fashioned terms of social determinism but in the new fashion of social discourse. No need to say what this inversion does to the old view of an artist, who brings his work over a threshold into beauty, nature transformed.

The Plotinian perspective is a hypothesis, a backdrop to thoughts, a way of looking at things. (I cannot disconnect the idea of perspective from that of hypothesis, cannot view any metaphysic as more—or less—than language at work in trial, letting different arrangements of existence appear through it.) Yet language hypotheses, like Kalymnos fishing nets, have a way of returning with catches—from each fresh cast. Catches—to crack the metaphor— are, in the present case, jointings, bridges, new fits of thought to thought, wholeness, indications. The Plotinian hypothesis—I feel in working with it—absorbs and bounds back into the major questions posed it. It enriches our life-growing sense of author, text, or artwork, and the medium they become from. Above all it clarifies a background, against which the life-swelling experiences of the threshold take new force. If that is my chief theme here, it is because the threshold is my first line of experience, the challenge life presents itself from inside—to grow more refined, just, and imaginative than it is.

From the Author's Undercabinet

The first two essays have cavorted. I have argued with example-chunks—after the style of anthology more than of logical constraint—for an implicitly Plotinian way of seeing the human situation. The first essay carried on without reference to that Plotinian zone but took a spiritual-monistic turn. I raised the issue of whether untranslatability exists, knowing that I ran a risk. By proving that such a category does not exist I would in a sense just be fulfilling an empty deductive chain. Nothing would be easier than to present examples, comment on their aspirations and failures, then conclude from their limited success that nothing can be decided about the impossibility of the undertaking. (Absolute possibility was, in fact, the aureole of this book-to-be, and I was prepared to follow that line even at risk.) But that first essay opened out discourse that surpassed the abstractness of its exercise. A logical point did, in the instance developed there, enrich itself by alternate formulation: we were jacked up to see that discontinuity—whether that of text with approaching understandings of it or of death with life that approximates it—cannot be argued from the inside, cannot be argued at all but can only be asserted.

This observation came into its energy in the second chapter, which swelled with the Plotinian model. I turned there to theories of the genesis of beauty, and my attention went largely to Adrian Stokes, who seemed to phrase a version of the Plotinian that went powerfully to the earth. Spiritual to the Ruskin degree, Stokes nevertheless found the greatness of art—as in the Malatesta temple—in the power of the artist to summon from the great voice of nature the song it longed to sing, and then—if the metaphor be forgiven—to raise this hosanna to some unidentified "on high." Maritain and Marcel—presenting Rilke—entered to reinforce this world model, into segments of which their sensibilities and thought fitted perfectly. In fact, the consensus, among the carefully chosen personnel of this discussion, became so great that I introduced dissonance for its own sake. Six thinkers of the mid–twentieth century were imported to show how deeply the Plotinian version, of artist-artwork-nature, tends to be slashed in our time. (Our time? A huge simplification. Of course Plato had already begun the assault on the Neoplatonic by his grouchy aesthetic, while ever since the Renaissance there has been consistent sniper fire directed at the whole-world image, spiritual monism, and its bevy of implications.) My final point, however, was that the implications of the anti-Plotinian are not yet in. Heisenberg, for one, worried the future, wondering what indeterminacy might determine from out of its own shifting center. Derrida, in arguing for play and shifting centers, argues for the continual deconstructing of the artwork's structure but at the same time—as I read him—allows that at each instant the reader establishes an identifiable and verifiable reading. There is stasis here, even though supplement is the cost of it. Even Foucault's view of the author function (to the extent it is not a modish trick) is full of the promise of a new perspective onto the powers that construct art—rather than a subversion of the oldest model. The chips are far from in on these newer readings of discontinuity, and we have no reason to reread in haste any of our older shapes.

Whatever vestige of the blithe there is in this posing of the Plotinian against the current and against attack will, as I have said, rest on this: that I am taking the Plotinian model as an hypothesis, an anthology of trial perceptions that can only certify itself by what happens in and to it. In the present interlude I offer, from the same standpoint, some material texts of my own making. (No point in calling them poems, even prose poems; for they are a kind of protoscience, as well as ontological work, by which they free material energies.) In the making and discovering of these artifacts, in the medium that becomes them, and in the kind of ostending I give them I find something of the Plotinian art model at work.

1

Matter is all over my legs. What's the matter with it? Doesn't it know how to behave? I reach down and take this matter and smear it over my body and grow softer; begin to like the feel. I make myself a matter coat and a matter hat, and go out preaching the virtues of matter. My only opponent is a guy named Spirit, who comes up to me in an alley and rubs against me. I rebuff him sternly. But some of him sticks to my gooey matter and grows in it. I'm covered with gray and white spores; roll on the sidewalk, try to quell the itching.

2

Soon I become conscious of a new sound in the garden. I ruffle through the tomatoes, poke in the stringbeans. The closer I get, the less I discover. Finally I decide it is the sound of growing. I retire to my kitchen. Once again however I hear a specific clawing. This time I stand and watch, wait for developments. At last I see a hand. It is clawing in the topsoil. Someone is imprisoned there. I run out to free him. But when I arrive the hand has vanished. The clawing sound has ceased. The earth is once more silent, over that body of longing.

3
I wash the minerals first
before putting them on the table.
My wife sets the peas down
gently in the midst of quartz.
My son surrounds the potatoes with bauxite.
Mealtimes, I say, are reminders
of a beautiful marriage
between the organic and the mineral.
I long to consume the mineral.
I wish my knife could cut into marble,
slicing it. I'd butter it carefully,
salt it, add a little paprika,
swallow it. From then on I'd eat nothing organic.
I'd nibble on the sides of mountains.
In me too the glistening patina
of minerals would grow hard and glossy.

Yet when I look around at the table
I see a row of grimaces,
the same old pull toward the organic,
the rotting passion of leafy spinach.

4

Matter is garlic—sweet, foul smelling—and attaches to me. I shower repeatedly, yet cannot dispel the odor. Then I go to a Spirit Source. He treats
me with imprecations. I watch my flesh grow drier, my hair sweeter. But
the garlic returns. Little by little my flesh grows foul again. I leap into the
river. This time my stench fouls the shores and the landscape. My Spirit
Source weakens. I squeeze myself like a pustule, until I am dry and lifeless,
a simple crush of peapod.

5

I aim my telescope at the core, peer down. Labyrinth rock-tubing. But
always some obstruction, just before I see to the end. I decide to crawl in,
wriggle through the opening, and make my way down from rock ledge to
magma. Just before the center I come to a crook that obstructs. I catch in
it and thrash. The more I agitate the tighter I stick. I prop myself on one
arm, peer down the tubing. What is that thrashing there? What obstructs
the center? I decide to crawl in, wriggle through the opening.

6

I raise my axe, carve into the slicey paste, and feel fossils deconstructing.
Then with Silurian tenderness I plunge in my hand, palp around for the
will of the material, discover a stone hand in mine. With care I extract this
fellow creature. It is my brother from the depths of my mind. I kiss him
passionately, then myself climb into the opened limestone and close it over
me. High above I hear my mind-brother coming closer, hacking a tough
path downward.

The Argument of Water

Tout ce que le coeur désire peut toujours se réduire à la figure
de l'eau.

Paul Claudel

Language bears the marks of the nature of man, its
maker. It is a notational system in which our psyche's free-fieldedness, organizational and problem-
solving powers, and care for resistance turn into being-in-the-word.
For Heidegger, "Sprache ist lichtend-verbergende Kraft des Seins
selbst," the point where man, in his *Ek-sistenz,* most characteristically surmounts the level of *das man,* ordinary impersonal speech.
Language is thus one of the effective and delightful human acts
and has been considered by many a human act that transcends the
human. The best of such judges, like Brice Parain, note that language is neither a reflection of "human emotions" nor a discourse
about "real things," but is "par sa nature une abstraction, en ce
sens qu'il ne manifeste pas la réalité, mais qu'il la signifie dans la
vérité." Parain's special use of *vérité* as distinct from the *réalité*
which things manifest is developed in his *Recherches sur la nature
et les fonctions du langage,*[1] and helps show us the peculiar freedom
language enjoys. The difficulty of his position is indicated by the
single word *abstraction,* which is forced on him because he insists
on viewing language epistemologically, not ontologically. Language is an abstract from reality; for Parain the *je* results from an
effort to provide knowledge about the empirical ego behind it. On

the whole, however, *je* results from nothing of the kind, but from its breathing origin's effort to do something organizational, caring, and freeing with the quality of its experience of itself; results from a state of affairs in being, an ontological condition.

This unitary view of language counteracts conceptions of literature that until recently were the norm but that within the last decades have weakened. These days many critical forces (linguistic, sociological, anthropological) are working to recuperate the vitality of the word (spoken or written) and the unity of all uses of it. These forces are threshold builders and discoverers, heralders whose traces are everywhere. Through them it has grown unfashionable to bow before the printed book, language in what Parain calls its "visage solennel." We have equally grown uneasy about the idea of "belles-lettres," a notion elaborated entirely in a privileged book-context and unthinkable in a preliterate society. (Even the creators of Greek culture never entertained the idea of a finer kind of writing. For Plato, a good poem, like a good saddle, was still a well-made artifact.) These are critical awarenesses that help us think back to the wholeness and oneness of uses of language.

We can test the actuality of this wholeness by selecting and bringing together some texts of several kinds, from widely separate periods: texts literary—in the usual sense—philosophical, scientific, and religious. I will try first to pay some attention to the distinction among such texts as they display different ways of dealing with the world. Only then will I examine their unity, though I will concentrate throughout on a single element of discourse, water.

Fifth Century before Christ

Original Taoism of the *Tao te ching* (sixth century B.C.), is as unencumbered with symbol as early Milesian thought and is even closer to the shape of the soul than the Greek work. A passage from the *Tao te ching:*

> 1 The best (man) is like water.
>   Water is good; it benefits all things and does not compete with

them.
It dwells in (lowly) places that all disdain.
5 This is why it is so near to Tao.
(The best man) in his dwelling loves the earth.
In his heart he loves what is profound.
In his associations, he loves humanity.
In his words, he loves faithfulness.
10 In government, he loves order.
In handling affairs, he loves competence.
In his activities, he loves timeliness.
It is because he does not compete that he is
14 without reproach.[2]

The details of the passage need little explanation, though its whole idiom is ineffable, Taoist. The *tao* itself means "way," "path," "order in things"; but the remainder of the vocabulary in the Chinese is limpidly and conventionally drawn from daily cultivated language. How does the passage run?

Only the first five lines concern "water." Lines 2–4 explain what water is and does, thus what the best man is "like"; then line 5 bridges explicitly from the geographic back into the moral. In a moment we are with the "best man" and his characteristics or his practices in action. What influence do we feel in these lines from the stated argument of water? Water, like the best man's soul, flows through lines 6–14: the bendingness, love, and humility of the man are all figures of water. Once it has been introduced, this argument forces the remainder of the passage to apply doubly: to the characterized man directly, and to that man as he is figured forth in the specific characteristics of water.

How does the metaphor of water enable the writer to say what he could not otherwise have said? We can draw on our common experience of water to support the definition of a particular kind of man. *Definition* usually means only "limit" and in that sense applies here, for we are enabled to draw the boundaries of a kind of man. But I think we mean more than that by *definition*. Water is in this connection not simply a metaphor *for* the best man, in which case it would be only a way of delimiting him; rather, man and water are mutually metaphorical, enliven and enrich each other. Man also means water. Water achieves a complicated figuring-forth of the significance of the best man. In this instance the figuring-forth could hardly have been achieved by any but an elemental projection.

Through means of language, man creates for himself a free-field in which he is able to propose and solve problems, appreciate some pleasures of distancing, delight in and shape various resistances. In all these exercises he moves out beyond the opaque, nontranscendent animal in himself and into the realm of the human, which he is thereby defining and creating. Does something like this occur in the manipulation of *water* in the present passage?

In one sense *water* has no existence here apart from that of the other words in the passage. On consideration, though, we can see that water and nothing else is behind *water,* and that the word is here doing work not shouldered by the other words in the passage. *Water* enlarges and thus frees the present argument: *the best man* is thereby opened out into the wider field of our experience and freed from meaning only what man prelinguistically is. This same enlargement of field involves immediate distancing because the items joined, "water" and "man," are unexpectedly joined, *unexpectedly* because drawn from a universe that, though intelligibly and naturally containing them both, rarely juxtaposes them. It follows, then, that a peculiar resistance is established between "water" and "the best man." This resistance here assumes its simplest form, emerging from the juxtaposition of substances. The resistance between "water" and "the best man" could only be explained as a qualitative form of their intelligible separation.

My second passage develops some of the implications of the first, using "water" as a means to understanding man; but the second passage couches its point in a greater and deeper darkness. It is from the *Vedanta-Sutras:*

> Water, when forming the seed of the body enters into the state of thinness, subtility, and herein again resembles faith, so that its being called *sraddha* (right reverence) is analogous to the case of a man who is as valiant as a lion being himself called a lion. Again the word *sraddha* may fitly be applied to water, because water is intimately connected with religious works (sacrifices, etc.) which depend on faith; just as the word "platform" is applied to men (standing on the platform). And finally the waters may fitly be

called *sraddha,* on account of their being the cause of faith, according to the scriptural passage, "Water indeed produced faith in him for holy works."[3]

Obviously the relation of water to *sraddha* is intimate, and each of the three points made here accounts for a different kind of closeness between the two principles. A certain opacity clouds much of the passage because we are not *certain* how literally we are supposed to take the discussion of water as faith. I suspect the problem is only ours and that the issue of literalness never arose for the writer. Water was probably, for him, exactly a kind of faith, just as the good is (still for us) exactly a kind of being higher than evil.

In the present passage, as in the Taoist, water is a good element. It is functioning, as in that earlier, to give sense to and receive from the notions of faith and *sraddha.* In both passages, similarly, man seems to be creating the same kind of semantic free-field, the same enlargement of experience, and the same possibility for calculated internal resistance among significant elements.

What does language—in such processes as we have seen at work in the use of *water*—what does language *do* to the world toward which it is a movement?

Human language is not about a world that is before it, that lies outside it and can be indicated by it, though language is always a constituting move out toward what we believe to be that world. The use of the expression *water* in the two passages above illustrates well for in neither place was mention of "water" part of a strong intention toward water in the empirical world. The clearly literary employment of the term *water* in these two passages might seem to leave no room for strong intention; but it has not excluded trace elements of a far more forceful explosion, the point at which world became relevant to these particular shapes in language. That point can be recovered either through a history of the term *water* or through a thorough history of these passages.

Consideration of the term *water,* here, shows that the source of the term is the dynamic and mastering approach to the element, water, which exists somewhere and somehow on the far side of its name. The negotiatory, clarificatory, and resistance-establishing principles that we see at work in the establishing of this particular passage are determinations of one general movement in existence, the movement from consciousness of phenomena out toward manipulable and essentialized representation of them. Naturally, *representation* is in this case a treacherous term. The word reaching for the world is longing to represent, but the system of notations created in this way is the world only by expectation.

My third introductory passage carries us into a different world of cultural experience, the Greek. The third fragment of Thales runs,

> The much-discussed four, of which we consider water the prime and somehow the single element, come into being for the unification and joining of earthly materials, in a mixture with one another.[4]

We find here some earlier sense of *water* as intimately continuous with what it means, with what, through mutual metaphoric relations, it enlivens. It seems plausible that the self-transformative power of water, which Thales mentions, had made itself plain to him in the rapid passage of water into mist, into rain, into snow, into ice; a labile process easily noticed on the Asia Minor coast. This sense controls his passage as clearly as it dominates in the Taoist or Vedic passages. Like the makers of those passages, Thales is transcending himself through a complex statement, a statement filled with his experience clarified and adapted to a new pattern of internal resistances.

The new note is somewhat hidden here, as is the whole tone of Thales' argument. We need to know that the Milesian philosophers were struggling to define a single first principle, that the much discussed four were water, air, the cosmic infinite (*to apeiron*), and fire, and that Thales was on record as considering water the center.

Water is the material cause (*arche*) of all things. This new note is special to Thales. His turn of mind was to center in on a single substance toward which language moves with much of its original integrity. The language-making process in Thales is as it always is, but the kind of transformation is different. Before too long Pindar will be able to say that

best of all things is water but gold, like a gleaming fire
by night, outshines all pride of wealth beside.[5]

For these Greeks *water* will have everything to do with whatever
can be made distinct and objectified in water.

During the fifth century no metaphorical factor was more
continuously used than water in the construction of cosmologies,
the affirming of ethics, or the substantiation of poetic visions. All
of these uses were developed and ramified. But many other re-
courses were available to the metaphorical machinery of the time.

In the Taoist and Vedic examples "water" is carried forward
by self into a renewing sense of the self's moral qualities. The moral
application is subliminal-theological in the *Vedanta-Sutras,* while
in the Taoist passage it is much more explicit, worked through as
an intuitional conceit. A beautiful analogy to the *Vedanta* passage
can be found in a parable from the philosopher Mencius on water
and the nature of man:

> Lao Tzu said: "The nature of man is like a swift current of water. If a breech
> is made to the east, it flows to the east; if a breech is made in the west, it
> flows to the west. And just as water is neither disposed to east nor west, so
> the nature of man is neither disposed to good nor to evil."

> Master Meng [Mencius] said: "It is true that water tends to flow neither
> to the east nor the west, but will it tend equally to flow upward and
> downward? Human nature tends toward goodness just as water tends to
> flow downward. There is no man who does not show tendency to be good;
> there is no water but flows downward. Now, by splashing water, you may
> cause it to fly over your head, and, by damming water, you may make it
> go up the hills. But is this the nature of water? It is, of course, external
> force that causes it to do so. Likewise, if a man does other than good, his
> nature is being forced in a similar way."[6]

That which in the Taoist passage on "water" is left to our feelings
about the nature of water is here worked out on an empirical-
logical level. Yet the appearance of rational coercion that Mencius
insinuates is only appearance; we are as clearly as in the Taoist
passage dealing with the rhetoric of experience. By the criteria of

physical science, "water" would, in either of these two passages, seem to have sacrificed any meaningful relation to water. But such a criterion would leave out the fact that "water"—in both the Taoist and Mencian passages—emerges from an empirical sense of water, and it would miss the point that such a sense is cast forth, given clarity, established syntactically, and used ("water" here being no more a metaphor for the moral situation in question than that situation is a metaphor for water, the terms in the arguments being interexplicative). This state of affairs sets the conditions for seeing how the two passages differ. The Mencian passage sets out to coerce, the Taoist to caress. The former has an intellectual and analyzable structure that is established by the synthetic imagination; the latter, the Taoist passage, feels its way along a simple intuitional line, equating a moral with a physical situation.

In the Zoroastrian *Shayast la shayast* we are still dealing with ways of negotiating forward into the word, yet we feel that much of the negotiation has been carried on prior to the writing down of what we find in the text, that the text is much less a working-through or a making-us-work-through than were the passages considered above. This is the preformed quality of language born from ritual.

There is here a religious sense both of the purity and of the corruptibility of "water." We read early in the *Shayast* of the great dangers of corrupting or polluting water. Throwing a corpse into water is the grossest defilement. A body rescued from water is to be placed at sufficient distance from the water so that drops will not flow back from the body into the water. Water was thought to be terribly sensitive, to be so easily upset a spirit that it should not even be looked at by the wrong person. A menstruous woman was not allowed to look at water, sit in water, walk in the rain. The distillation passage that follows simply applies this whole set of proscriptions to a sinner:

> And when he has committed sin against water, even . . . against a single drop of it, and has not atoned for it, that also stands up as high as the plants stood, and does not let him go to heaven.[7]

Like the Taoist and Mencian passages, this one bases itself on the rhetoric of conviction, uses "water" as vehicle of argument; yet here water has become an *object* of concern in instruction. The tone is new (though it is not yet at all the tone in which water, for Thales and Pindar, remained in language an object of ikonic concern). "Water" is now an object of concern rather than of internalized perception or of discrete objectification. Yet "water" is still an element in transcendence, a creation by resistance as well as by distancing and movement into an open field.

"Resistance" is inherent in man's first counteracting of his body's parallel relation to the ground, in his first standing up. It is not easy to see the resistance principles of language making in operation; it is easier to see the desire either for making a free-field or the desire for distancing. Yet these three efforts through language fit tightly together and help to make one another visible. What has happened in the transcending of mere sense through language to make possible the ritual passage about sinning against water? Religious sensibility and system have gone to work on the experience of what they call *water*, and have done several things with that experience: have loosed it from the determinations and constrictions attaching to water-understood-as-a-part-of-the-physical-world; and thus have freed it for human use. Religious sensibility and system have at the same time removed, from what they find to be water, that pressure on us that is exerted by all immediate, unmediated objects of perception; by all the things that, while they constitute our worlds, act on us as forcefully as we on them. Finally religious sensibility and system have given as well as taken away. They have given to the linguistic syntax containing water-as-"water" both coherence and the preconditions for granting meaning. It is this last aspect, the meaning-endowing aspect, that makes the establishment of resistance a step of peculiar value to us. Are not *water, plants,* and *heaven* joined in our present passage, in a dense intelligibility that we could never directly experience into the awareness, beyond those words, of the world toward which they are reaching? The achieved effect is partly just distancing and humanization; but it is equally a setting-into-relation of parts that had previously been scattered over the world. That new collocation is itself a model of resistance, of the way in which man works through his language to press a texture out from himself against the world. "Water" and the features of man's "inner existence" are similarly joined in the Taoist and Mencian passages.

The moral use of "water" can be briefly illustrated by two more passages that take us farther into the cleansing and therapeutic sense of the element. The first is from "The Story of Sumedha," a tale allegedly related by the Buddha to his disciples, telling how, "in his long-ago existence as the Brahman Sumedha, he first resolved to strive for the Buddhaship":

> Even as a man befouled with dung,
> Seeing a brimming lake at hand,
> And nathless bathing not therein
> Were senseless should he chide the lake;
>
> So, when Nirvana's lake exists
> To wash away corruption's stain,
> Should I not seek to bathe therein,
> I might not then Nirvana chide.[8]

Man as moral element is here brought closer to "water" than in any of our other passages. Nirvana is usually pictured as less tangible even than water, while here it is an immediate presence given its own life by the corruption of the "I," which thirsts to be cleaned. There is suddenly no possibility of taking water as a metaphor *for* some moral state; the water is the moral state. There is that minimum shuffling that is required in any working out of the moral in terms of things, but the name *water* is so thoroughly moralized that it exists in the language as almost diaphanously ethical. Freeing, distancing, syntactical preparation are all at work on the term here; this "water" means a great deal to us. The lake is still recognizably carried forth from the world of the "real" lake.

A comparable passage makes a moral identification through "water," laying little stress on syntactical resistance. It is drawn from a Japanese text and is said to come from the Buddha's mouth:

The mind, therefore, like a waterfall, never ceases its activity. Just as a peaceful ocean suddenly becomes a tumult of waves because of some passing tempest, so the Ocean of Mind becomes stirred by tempests of delusion and winds of karma. And just as the ocean again becomes peaceful when the tempest passes, so the Ocean of Mind resumes its natural calm, when the winds of karma and delusion are stilled.[9]

"Water," here, is more intimate to mind than "water" was to man or faith in the Taoist, Brahmanic, or Mencian passages. The mind-element identification is plainer here even than in "The Story of Sumedha." There the "I" longed for the cleansing lake, destroying in its longing almost all the syntactical interpositions that formal imagery tended to establish. The formal apparatus of imagery appears in the present passage: the "just as" in two places alerts us to the difference and rapprochement of the elements to be compared. But for a reason at first unsuspected, the difference is eradicated as soon as it is established. Mind is accepting and transcending itself through the passage. In working through this account of its identity with the ocean within itself, it flows naturally over, through, and around the themes of the argument. At the end, our minds close over the whole intimacy of the argument and thus reenact the specific passage described here, passing through distinction and delusion back into the unity of themselves.

The freeing effect of "water" could hardly be more decisive than it is here. Such an awareness gave Thales a first principle.

A last passage from the Far East will bring us back toward Thales and the Greek world:

The Buddha said: "You should ponder on the fact that, though each of the four elements (earth, moisture, heat and vapour) of which the body is made up has a name, they none of them (constitute any part of) the real self. In fact, the self is non-existent, like a mirage."[10]

Water joins the argument along with the other elements, along with the rest of the outer-phenomenal world. Or can we equally say, with the rest of the inner-phenomenal world? The elements compose the body that, though distinct from the "real self," is still, in Buddhist psychology, the matrix of impressions, dreams, anxieties, and other traits of inner awareness. The elements reach toward self but break against the paradoxical nonexistence of selfhood, a nonexistence that in Buddhism is supreme existence.

What is the Buddha doing with "water"? We find here the result of reflection and logical analysis. The truth of this argument has been established long before the present writing down of it. In that, the passage resembles Thales' observations on water, and oddly enough the point made here also returns us to Thales. Yet there is an instructive difference. The path in Thales is toward the incorruptible lodged *in* the elements, especially in water; while for the Buddha elements like water tend to be simply defining conditions, which help us to understand how different from all such elements is what is perfect in us.

Two of our passages, from Thales and the Buddha (the last cited), show considerable interest in water as a supposedly component element of the world and of ourselves in the world. They are cosmological observations, the Greek moving farther toward the attitude of natural science than the Indian text, which interests itself in the elements so it can stress the character of the self, the characterless vehicle toward perfection. The Taoist passage on water and the best man and the Buddhist passage on the mind as waterfall or calm ocean both use water and self as interexplanatory metaphors, as ways of making us feel the ultimate translucency of what we are. The Vedic passage on *sraddha* and water makes the same moral claim, though with more apparatus of logical coercion. Perhaps the platform of prejudgment from which so many Vedic statements take off makes for this passage's doctrinal tenor. The Mencian passage on the directionality of "water" also makes a logical claim, drawing the tendency of flowing water into the same thought with the inherent moral tendency of man. That logical claim clearly has to do with the relation of "water," not of water, to human being. The most primal of the passages is that from the *Shayast la shayast*, concerning the easy corruptibility of water. It is a valuable reminder of how little involvement there is between fifth-century religious experience across the civilized globe and the religions, or religious language-worlds, of superstition and dark subliminal forces. There is some of this "darkness" in Vedic thought, especially in the earliest Vedas and Upaniṣads where struggles between Aryan and indigenous gods are working themselves out. But there is little of the numinous in Greek thought or in the Far Eastern religions. The strongly numinous marks later forms of those cultures—the Eleusinian spirit in Greece, the Tantric in Buddhist life, or syncretic, local-deity growths within Confucianism and Taoism. But in the thought of the fifth century B.C., elemental experience is handled with a high degree of projection and control. The Adrian Stokes discussed earlier has written on just this point in treating the clarity of figures of the ego in classical Greek thought and creation, and I think we could extend the point with surprising accuracy to the Far East of that day. Some lost darkness was reintroduced into water and "water" by the Christian fathers.

The Rhetoric of Christianity

The larger thresholds of this essay will expose themselves at the contact points between the religious-philosophical—which pervades these fifth-century texts—and those lyrical or scientific texts that I will discuss later. We will concentrate later on the possibilities of converting water-language from one domain into another. First, though, we need to drink deeper at the wells of premodern language, particularly from the rhetoric of Christianity, religious but, like the fifth-century idiom, at every point susceptible to the scientific.

First, a passage drawn from the Manichaean tradition (third century A.D.) involving the eternal conflict between the forces of light, life, living water, and those of darkness, death, foul or turbid water. The dualism of this thought separates it from the Christian sense of water, but the Manichaean sense of the meaningful mystery *in* water is akin to the Christian sense. We read, in fragments, the following Manichaean passages:

> They brought living water and poured it into the turbid water; they brought shining light and cast it into the dense darkness. They brought the refreshing wind and cast it into the scorching wind.

> As it entered the turbid water, the living water lamented and wept. . . . As he mingled the living water with the turbid, darkness entered the light.[11]

Most of these examples deal with "water" as an element in analogy, as a notion around which to arrange an argument. The passage I earlier termed *primal* was from a Persian text, the *Shayast la shayast,* in which the purity of the water was at stake. There was a great deal of mystery in "water," which brought us experientially into itself with flow and urgency. That very power pointed to a general trait of fifth-century pre-Christian language, that it expressed and exercised a strongly dominating, cleanly cut global grasp of the world of experience.

How does the experience of water operate in the present Manichaean passage? Some context may help us reply. Hans Jonas provides the following accounts of the two kinds of water:

> Living water: flowing water, which is of sublime origin and flows in streams, all of which the Mandaeans called "Jordans." . . . This alone can be used ritually, i.e., for the frequent baptisms which are a main feature of the Mandaean cult. For this reason the Mandaeans can only settle close to rivers. The expression "living water" is probably taken over from the Old Testament. . . . The opposite is stagnant water and the troubled waters of the sea.

> Turbid water. Troubled water, lit. "water of the Abyss (of Chaos)"; the original matter of the world of darkness with which the living water mingled.[12]

The people for whom these definitions apply are the Mandaeans, "a sect which survives in a few remnants in the region of the lower Euphrates (the modern Iraq), no less violently anti-Christian than anti-Jewish, but including among its prophets John the Baptist in opposition to and at the expense of Christ."

The two Mandaean passages are bound to their immediate environments, yet suggest something general of the complex relation between language-world and the dynamic operations—releasing, freeing, submitting to a fresh syntactical control—that are the axes of language making.

Each account of these passages is a way of answering the

question, How does the demand of experience operate here? A phenomenological account seems to present itself first and is essentially the diction adopted up to this point. "Water" is here freed from the conditions of sense awareness into at least the state of being named. "Water" has been brought into relation with elements of experience, with "light" and "darkness," with which it usually enjoys only the most casual relationships. "Water" has simultaneously been given a freedom within the new syntax of relationships through which we transcend and define ourselves— this power to be part of our transcendence being part of "water's" own new definition. That new definition is the phenomenological account of the demand of experience in these passages.

Another kind of account is possible that we might call *psychological* and that extends our explanatory apparatus. The "psychological" account is more abstract than the phenomenological and can take many forms; is plastic in its distance from and its loose relation to language phenomena. A depth psychology of the present passages might consider our relation to the waters of the womb, of urine, of breast milk, and the evaluations we attach to those fluids as we grow up with and through them. Existential psychoanalysis would take more interest in the way we live our senses of those fluids in unique existential situations. In both cases the psychological account would go "out beyond" the primary phenomena of language. It would transcend the phenomenological account, showing how the demand of experience operates, how it dramatizes psychic awareness latent in us.

The Mandaean passage makes a psychic demand. Jung, Neumann, and Rank have plumbed some of our deep senses of water, and we know from how far under the surface of literature those senses rise. But this knowing exists in relation to the phenomenological world. Depth psychology, to the degree it finds out what we are sublingually, cannot finally clash with phenomenological accounts of mind in language.

We can follow these extending distinctions along a course that flows:

> Having warned a certain righteous man, with his three sons, together with their wives and their children, to save themselves in an ark, He sent a deluge

of water, that all being destroyed, the purified world might be handed over to him who was saved in the ark, in order to a second beginning of life.[13]

Here the water of purification resembles the living water of the Mandaeans. Linguistic freeing and resistance-establishing rhythms assert themselves, moving "out into" the psychological.

We are offered various awarenesses: of the overflowing of waters, the cleansing through those waters, and the destined vehicle that cleaves and finally survives the menace of waters, that survives touched by, and safely beyond, those waters. By all these awarenesses we bring into existence various latent traces of experience, traces so representative we want to call them archetypal. The term *archetypal* has often compromised itself in discussions of language and literature. A book like Maud Bodkin's *Archetypal Patterns in Literature* contents itself, for all its archetypes, with a random assortment of themes and motifs, a mine of applied associations. But the notion of *archetype* is not useless if we think of archetypes as general thematic patterns lodged deep in psychic life; as patterns which experience in phenomena can activate.

How do such archetypal activations mesh with the dynamic operations of distancing and free-field making, which we discussed above? The establishment of a free-field and the creation of new humanly flavored inner syntax have been seen to lie at the center of language making, at least under phenomenological consideration. Freedom, a sense of controlled openness, has been humanly established in the language-work. Does something different from this happen in the depths of psyche when channels of immediate, deep, and dramatic experience are opened out into our nature? The awarenesses triggered by what we called *archetypes* escape through and from themselves as releases. But with this one crucial difference, that volition plays a much more vigorous role in establishing a world through language than in shaping archetypal awarenesses that language will activate and use. Those awarenesses are coefficients of our negotiation with culture. But because they are first of all channels and channeled, they are, to a degree, bound. The making of language itself, we see by the phenomenal account, is limited by choice alone. It can use the psychic reservoir. The phenomenal account, by holding close to this pure immediacy of the language act, is closer to it than is the psychic account, which in a sense strikes *below* the required level of organization. Both accounts will enable us to see thresholds at which one type of language—scientific, poetic, theological—finally declares its affiliation (if not its identity) with another.

A variety of Christian and post-Christian texts will keep the foregoing method-questions in sight, and will finally justify whatever discoveries we achieve into the threshold-crossing potential of diverse types of language. First the topic of the "righteous man" and the waters he crosses, picked up from 1 Peter:

> Because Christ also died once for our sins, the just for the unjust, that he might offer us to God, being put to death indeed in the Flesh, but enlivened in the spirit. In which also coming he preached to those spirits that were in prison: which had been some time incredulous, when they waited for the patience of God in the days of Noah, when the ark was a building: wherein a few, that is, eight souls, were saved by water. Wherein baptism, being of the like form also saveth you.[14]

The last line helps us bridge to baptismal waters. It also alerts us to the ramification of elemental terms in the early Christian language system. The waters of flood are forever flowing into those of baptism.

The preaching of Christ to the spirits—evidently those bound in the Abyss and met by Our Lord on his descent into the Underworld—was an address to offspring of the Devil; just as today, in the world of this passage, Christ must address the fallen world through baptism. In both cases He intervenes; in both cases water is introduced as being, or having been, the source of salvation. It is of special beauty that "waiting" is here introduced as motif, the flood caught in that waiting's power of attention. The force of that effect is enhanced by the detail that precisely eight souls were saved.

This is a passage of more symbolic involvement than any previously considered, a passage in which the nominal details—"water," "spirit," "death"—withdraw even farther than those in the previous passages from the outer world they imply beyond themselves. Similarly, the openness of the free-field created by this language is more intellectually mobile than had previously been the case. The ideas working through this passage are supple and pregnant, the system of resistances among words proving to be asymmetrical, isolating, and creative.

The psychological component is found interweaving with the phenomenal. The establishment both of freed elements and of a free-field for syntactical organization, as we see it at work here, is parallel to breakthrough into a freedom in the experience of the passage.

The argument of water dominates this passage, which is dense, even cluttered, and which the commentator Bellarmine considered among the most difficult in the Bible. Like many such difficult segments, this one draws together two institutions—here flood and baptism—that can only be joined in a kind of invasion by feelings, a psychic entrance that at once traps itself in a labyrinth of unsureness and restraints. How are the waters of baptism and of the flood, as sacred and saving, to be coexperienced? To answer is to work through the syntax of the passage, determining the *relation* of "flesh" to "spirit," of "spirit" to "souls," of "water" to the "soul," of "baptism" and the "flood" to "water." I use the term *relation* in an unusual sense, meaning simply to take the notion of syntax literally and seriously and to press it hard. It is through such syntax, experienced as resistance, that the course of our experiential meeting with the text *is* and the going-forth psyche *becomes*.

A religious tradition, like the Christian, gains by letting the key nouns of its argument flow into one another, passage after passage, institution after institution, down the centuries, during which language acquires an aging and deepening, a final adequacy to one entire verbal stance. Maximum syntactical density and maximum earned freedom can only be achieved in this way.

For texts touching baptism, I will choose only two. The first picks up the theme of Old Testamental aquatic experience and relates it again to the mysteries of Christian experience in baptism. This time the context is the crossing of the Red Sea by the Jews and their initiatory rite through water:

> First, when the people had been sent forth from Egypt, and having crossed the waters escaped the Egyptian king's wrath, the waters swallowed up the

king himself with all his troops. What clearer image could there be, of the sacrament of baptism? The nations are freed from the temporal—through water that is—and the devil, our original master, they left submerged under the waters.[15]

The emphasis is on the movement through "water," and on the sense in which "water" can both purify and annihilate. It is noteworthy that the sense of transgression and progression through water can carry the heavy burden of relating experiences widely separate in time and context. Water is known far down in us. In that sense, crossing water is so inevitably crossing ourselves that it floods all chronological dykes.

This baptismal passage bespeaks the transformation of movement through waters and thus ties itself to an archaic sense of water as purifying. The second baptismal passage invokes an equally ancient sense of water—as spiritually protean. In this case too, the emphasis is on a transformation, on water as a transformation of itself. It is a familiar turn of the early Christian imagination:

> The bitterness of the water was changed and the water made fresh and drinkable by Moses' staff. This wood was none other than Christ himself who transformed the waters of baptism.[16]

The transformative archetype works so powerfully on us here that we accept both the daring historical conflation of Moses and Christ and the grotesque fusion of Christ first into his cross and then into Moses' staff. How has language working through our sense of water accomplished this?

By a psychological account we can give an explanation at one remove from the texture of the passage. Looking to Jung, we see how deeply the awareness of the aquatic in us is our awareness of how things, parts of an experienced world, flow into each other, how readily they abandon their temporal or spatial contours. We have mentioned how nicely language utilizes these deep potentials of awareness, how it leads them into earned freedoms. The phenomenological account shows us more clearly, with more detail of presentation, just what is happening here. The energies in "water" are being negotiated into a field of freedom where "water" can be brought into conjunction with elements like "staff" and "wood," and with the typological overtones of these elements. The ground of this feeling and syntactical reorganization is so completely what-we-are-as-animals-making-language that it cannot occur to us to test the made product by standards of probability other than its own.

I have been viewing "water" as principle of salvation, as self-transmutative and purifying. I added psychological accounts of the experience of "water" to the phenomenological accounts with which the essay began, and we tried to suggest how the latter accounts are closer than the former to what-goes-on-in-the-mak-ing-of-language. I want now to turn the argument away from the experience of water as part of an instituted situation—*fluminal* or baptismal—to its place in the most haunting and longing-filled tale of medieval Christianity, the legend of the Holy Grail. We come at once onto a certain Christian sense of water as alter-nately purifying and corruptible, or rather as purifying because corruptible.

For the Middle Ages, the Roman soldier whose lance opened a source of blood and water in Christ's side, opened a flood of new elemental meanings for ritual and art; we know from the inner development of other aquatic language, in flood and baptismal thought, how readily this new flowing would be channeled. We sense the beginning of the movement in parts of a passage in Origen:

> The Lord standing in the temple said: "Let him who thirsts come and drink in water the power of grace" (John 7:37). Similarly, when the people in the desert were suffering the dangers of thirst, Moses took up a wand, a staff that is, and struck a rock with it, and fountains of water flowed forth: in this way he was indicating the origin of the sacrament of baptism. That the rock existed as a form of Christ is proven by the blessed apostle when he says: "For they drank from a spiritual rock, which rock was Christ" (I Corinth. 10:4). So there is no doubt but what that rock had the form of the Lord's body; which, struck by the lance, poured forth living water to the thirsting, as it was written: "Rivers will pour forth from his belly" (John 7:38). . . . And then those waters, brought forth from the rock, rivers flowing broadly from the side of Christ, revealed by a typical prefiguration. Who does not know that when our Lord, a source of the water of life, a

source spurting into eternal life, that when our Lord hung from the wood of the cross, not only did blood pour from the wound in his side, but a great flowing current of water poured, showing forth that his bride, the Church, arose from his side like the first humans, like Eve who came from Adam's rib, and that thus the Church had two baptisms, one of water, one of blood.[17]

The passage joins several central medieval negotiations through water: Christ as the rock from which Moses' rod struck water, Christ from whose belly waters will pour, Christ as the cross from whose side water as well as blood flowed, the association of the water of baptism with this last outpouring. Whatever in water is most nourishing and fertile is being drawn here into a principle as broad as the Christian experience.

Of special interest is the contextual power this experience of water brings to bear on the water that the Roman soldier's lance released. All the "waters" in this passage and in this system of experience and thought flow together in language and in the self-transcendence that occurs through this language. The water is struck from Christ's side as water had been struck from rock, though now a lance replaces a rod. The water from Christ's side pours forth with largeness of gesture, seems continuous with the gesturing toward Mary and the new Church in the same way that Eve, female like the Church, was brought to birth from the first man's side. Christ as the water of life is being understood in terms of all these manifestations of himself as water. The network is elaborate and profound. What account can we give of it?

First there is the unusual syntactical density. The system of inner resistance is more obvious than the achievement of freedom through language, or the opening that freedom acquires for itself. That resistance introduces a new qualitative texture into language. The water struck from Christ's side is given a peculiar quality—a density and character—that draws part of its own character from the qualities of the other waters in the passage. Those qualities are carefully juxtaposed to one another. In each case a container or hollow with water in it is pierced, and the fluid released. Each container is different, but the releasing gesture, the movement into each, is similar. The controlled difference in similarity strengthens the qualitative fabric. With each added factor the earlier elements coalesce so that the notion of container, savior, and released water is enriched to quadruple complexity by the end of the passage. Syntactic resistance is the counterplay between distinct experiential elements and their final union in such a passage.

This system of resistances is related to the free-field of language and, at an earlier stage, to the freeing of the world from itself through language. By the free-field of language I mean the establishment of the kind of density through which we can transcend ourselves into what we are significantly not yet, into what we have not yet come to be. Such self-transcendence is a real move into the open or at least an establishment of new channels of motion in the being of which we are at the same time being ourselves. It is the going out into and becoming, the uncharted possibility named by the experience of the diverse awarenesses of water evoked by this passage. As a "going out," it is at the same time intimately linked to the emergence by which the word is distinguished from the thing, act, or relationship to which it will henceforth refer. "Water" is free. In two senses it is free of any compulsion; it has to behave itself only under certain broad conditions of *vraisemblance*; it *can* absorb into itself implications of every variety—religious, poetic, or natural-scientific. (It is in such cases language's insistence on its potential wholeness.) What has occurred to it in the present passage is just that kind of absorption.

In approaching the Grail, we stopped at a passage concerning—in a complex and exfoliating way—the effluence from the side of the dying Christ. That passage from Origen is significant for the aquatic thinking of Christian theology since any appreciation of the Grail legend requires understanding the detail of Christ's dying, which lay behind and haunted those legends. The elaborated Grail story—as we see in Marx, *Le graal*—is shot through with folklore motifs. But those motifs, say of the dying king in a fairy palace and of that king's virile successor, collect themselves around a stabilizing axis of Christian history.

I want to take two texts from a point much farther on in the story. Each is drawn from among the events that transpire at the palace of the sick ruler—the Fisher King—that ruler who possesses the Grail but who is dying, and around whom the waters are wasting. The first passage concerns the water of despond; the second the contents of the Grail that Joseph of Arimathea had rescued after the Last Supper.

In the first passage Chrétien de Troye's Perceval approaches the water that separates him from the castle of the Fisher King:

> He goes along the shore until he approaches a rock, and the water touches that rock so that he could not go forward. At once he saw on the water a boat which was coming from upstream: there were two men in the boat. He stops, and waits for them and thinks that they would go until they came up to him. They both stopped; they remain quiet in the middle of the water, for they had anchored themselves very well; and the one who was in front was fishing with a line and was baiting his hook with a small fish little larger than a grayling. He who passes, greets them, and asks them: "Teach me," says he, "lords, if there is in this water either ford or bridge?" He who is fishing answers him: "None, brother, by my faith, nor is there any boat, believe me in this, larger than the one in which we are, which would not carry five men, twenty leagues upstream nor down, so one can not get a horse across, for there is neither ferry nor bridge nor ford."[18]

The water of this passage is, from the sensuous point of view, more watery than that of any passage we have yet read. This water is still, slow, faintly menacing, not so much for what is said of it as for what can or cannot take place on it. It seems a substance of dangerous, and nearly deathlike, viscosity. It is a special substance and compels us with its own aura.

There is here an almost ikonic emphasis on "water," on the creation of a new free-field, and on the establishment of a notational realm through which the user of these notes can transcend himself. All these items are in the present passage difficult to isolate and penetrate. The term *water*, as we see it in the lines two, three, and six of this translation, is much more nearly a function of the other words in the passage than the term *water* has been in earlier passages. Here language summons up an aquatic mood, holds it before us as something morally important and suggestive, adequate to our entry and transcendence. Such an aquatic mood is sharply distinct from the mood established by the "water" operative in the previous passage from Origen. In Origen, water has been apprehended, taken under control, been made a concept. It has little materiality. In the present passage language rises toward sense, matter into a materiality of its own.

The last Grail text fits here in a far more familiar and man-ageable way. This is from the Grail legend as told by Robert de Boron; the speech on the Grail itself is by Petrus:

> For no one will see the Grail,
> Or so I think, that will not find it agreeable:
> It will please all,
> It will be agreeable to all, and will make life beautiful for all;
> Seeing it will be as great a delight
> For those who will endure to be with it
> And use its companionships
> As the relief the fish finds
> When, while held in a man's hand,
> It can escape from the hand
> And can go swimming in the great water.[19]

Again, context matters, this being a story, but not as in the pre-ceding passage. In this piece the sense of oceanic immensity is given full control, allowed to carry the liquid of the chalice out to the full extent of human awareness.

I have referred off and on to some characteristics of syntactical density, that profound trait of man's language. Within that density we have seen several examples of fusion among the terms denoting water: in passages from Thales and the Buddha, and in the passages from 1 Peter, Tertullian, and Origen. In the trinitarian notion of the contents of the Holy Grail, we can see a literal application of this view of the self-transformative inner power of water. In the same way—in arguments about transubstantiation—orthodox theologians came during the Reformation to defend the physically transformable powers of water or wine. If alchemical thought, which centered on elemental transformations, had centered on water, we would have found supreme examples of "water" altered in nature. As it is, though, the alchemical examples fall just short of this expectation. Some examples from the literature of alchemy suggest the character of its discussions of water, prepare us for considerations of science in a stricter sense.

First, an introductory passage from Aristotle's *Meteorologica* in which, following his general distinction between matter and form and his belief that matter can endure any form, he views water as the physical origin both of fossils (minerals) and metals. Moisture below the earth, he has said, exhales itself in two principal forms, one vaporous, the other smoky; to which exhalations there correspond two kinds of bodies that originate in the earth, the "fossil" and "metals."

> The dry exhalation is that which by burning makes all the "fossil" bodies, such as the kind of stones that cannot be melted, realgar and ochre and ruddle and sulphur and such other things. . . . The vaporous exhalation is the cause of all metals, fusible or ductile things, such as iron, copper, gold. For the vaporous exhalation being shut in, makes all these things, and especially when in stones. . . . Hence these things are water in a sense, and in a sense not. For the matter was that of water potentially, but it is no longer, nor are they from water which has been changed through such affection, such as are juices.[20]

We are with the intermutability of the elements, a theme that for the alchemists was to become a topic of endless "practical" investigation, as it is again in our nuclear researches; but which is important for the present argument because it poses the notion of water as continuous with the other elements. It poses that notion intellectually, as Thales had raised it, but after a fashion destined to arouse strong feelings among the alchemists.

At this point, water has begun to pass into "water" under conditions resembling at least a protoscientific operation. We have already seen examples of the use of water both as element and form, for moral or religious argument. In some of those passages, say in the one attributed to Thales, emphasis fell on the sense of water as outside and experientially distanced. In forthcoming examples of early modern—sixteenth- and seventeenth-century—scientific writing about water, we will come on the clear sense of water as a distanced outside object. But Aristotle's account of water already suggests the new perception. "Water," in the concluding lines of the passage, is an abstraction from human concerns. It exists beyond or outside those concerns as a matter through which, once it has been "termed," we may be able to transcend ourselves in quite a special way; but which invites us to go out to it rather than to move in through it. In this it operates differently from the water through which we saw the men fishing in the river before the castle of the Fisher King. That water remained intact in all its sensual integrity.

No such impression is left by the high period of alchemical language, where nothing is untransformed by the mystique—often the actual magic—of humanizing thought. The astounding bravura of that thought can be suggested by a little statement, an ejaculation:

Mare tingerem si mercurius esset!

I would tinge the sea if it were made of mercury![21]

This line is attributed to the pseudo-Lully, a writer of the twelfth or thirteenth century. Mercury is the ruddy element, which, in transforming processes effected by the philosopher's stone, can release its latent color and latent nature. This outcry uses the sea to talk about the immensity of what the alchemist could effect if his object were the right one. But Lully does not use the sea here only as an element of imagery, as part of a verbal-literary reinforcement. Water, as all the alchemists knew, was a crucial base element in alchemy; and so its powers were in some sense the final form of the whole operation for which intermutability was *the* essential principle. That sense of alchemy's founding substance surely colored the argument of the whole science.

The alchemists called water *theion hudor,* holy water, a substance that seems to have been a product of distillation. This water, according to F. S. Taylor in *The Alchemists,* "had the power of acting upon metals, corroding or coloring them. The name divine water was evidently applied to the yellow calcium polysulphide solution made by boiling lime, sulphur, and water; also to mercury, and to yellow dye-liquors used for superficial tinting. Zosimus, in fact, uses the word as a generic term for all liquids useful in the Art." (Mercury could be dyed by *this* water, which was, in a sense, the sea that Lully would have wanted to dye.) It is this water that the alchemist Bonnellus, writing in the early seventeenth century, refers to:

> You must realize that our water is no commonplace water, but enduring water [*eau permanente*]; which never ceases the search for its mate [the *feu secret* of alchemical reaction]; which mate it seizes instantly upon finding it; and these two substances become one substance.[22]

The magic of humanizing thought has touched this water, though this magic is in touch with thingliness. It is a much less abstract water, here, than we found in Origen and Tertullian, or in most of our pre-Christian passages. This *eau permanente* can join in marriage, is restless and seeking and, like a good chemical reagent, leaps for its chemical mate. It prefigures the far less dramatically personified chemical elements on which the first modern chemists lavished much verbal enthusiasm. Much of high alchemical thought occupies just this position, verging in toward the language of early science, yet remaining more sensually poetic than scientific water. Is alchemical language the threshold between the vernaculars of religion and science?

The notion of water as sacred has met us in the *Shayast la shayast* passage and in one drawn from Mandaean culture, and we find it again in the Bonnellus passage—where it fuses with the alchemist's use of language. The trope's shape is the same as before: a rhythm of releasing "water," shaping a syntax in which "water" can be understood relationally and promoting through the density of that syntax a kind of emergence of ourselves through ourselves. All this—within the context of alchemical rhetoric—is to be found in the present passage; as is that moving toward freedom in psychological terms, which is here gratified in the sudden fusing of the two kinds of water. Yet there is in the passage before us a peculiar quality of "presenting the element," a holding or adorational gesture, marked off by the noteworthy *nostre* of the first line; and this ikonic quality marks off the passage from most of those we have considered earlier.

The same applies to the discussion of "water" in parallels between the holy mass and alchemical rites. Such parallels were emphasized by the alchemists to confirm their respectability and to engage with the highest mysteries of the day. Here is one alchemical formula that seems to pick up a line from the Roman liturgy. On Holy Saturday the priest plunges the Easter candle into water, saying,

May it descend into this fullness of the font, as a power of the Holy Spirit.

Very similar, Canseliet points out, is "la prière que prononce Melchior Ciboniensis penché sur l'incroyable réalisation de l'accord définitif entre les deux éléments contraires" (water and spirit):

> O sublime source, from which the true water of life will truly spring, as the reward of your faithful. Alleluia![23]

The spiritualizing of H_2O could hardly be more dramatic or sensuous. The formula is pronounced by a celebrant bent over holy water, in a gesture carried directly into language.

Early Science

There is a way of using elemental experience and language that has become more than familiar, that has become a manner of being-in-the-world. I mean the scientific way, a fixed habit of trying to let things in the world be, of trying to give an account of things without significantly distorting their natures. Despite the inroads of idealistic and critical philosophies from Kant to our day, this scientific ideal persists. It persists in the face of Heisenberg's insistence that even the equipment with which the scientist measures disturbs what he measures. Yet despite that ideal, the language of science remains but a threshold away from those of earlier religious and naturalistic thought. Our remarks on alchemy have shown one path across the Bering Strait, one step onto the threshold.

The more neutral languages of water try to turn away from the inward gestures studied above, as well as from the ethical uses some pre-Christian texts made of water. Of course, we did see the beginning of a "neutral" notion of water in Thales and Aristotle. But that was the merest beginning. From the seventeenth century on, scientific perspective takes over the field of aquatic prose. The *eau permanente* of the alchemists is itself transmuted by what will become the various waters—heavy, nitrous, ferruginous—of the contemporary scientist.

Water, in that newest scientific language, is more directedly and extravertedly referential than are nouns like *water* in the passages from Confucius, Lao Tzu, or Origen. It is not that *water* as the contemporary scientist employs the term is more like water than is *water* as the theologian or poet uses it. Strictly and literally all nouns are equally unlike what they name, are radically metaphors. But the scientists' proper nouns are both ikons in themselves and a reaching toward what they name, the noun of scientific discourse above all looking out and doing so with an intention to point, to draw attention outward from itself. The *water* of Origen's passage on the other hand is an invitation toward the interiority of the language world. That essential minimum of difference is here, to assure that the threshold between contemporary physics and theology is not casually shuffled across.

The scientific use of language is plain in any modern textbook, though fully to understand it would mean going into the ultimate assumptions of scientific theory. The earlier stages of scientific thought in the sixteenth and seventeenth centuries are instructive in this respect, because there we can see the emergence of a language of science from the language, say, of alchemy. Newton writes,

> Water has no great power to dissolve because it rejoices [*quia pauco acido gaudet*] in little acid; for we call acid what attracts and is attracted strongly. For we see things that are dissolved in water dissolve slowly and without effervescence.

And a few lines farther in the same treatise, *De natura acidorum:*

> Water cannot be compressed because its parts are contiguous, while air can be since its parts do not yet touch each other, but if they did, air would turn into marble.[24]

The *eau permanente* or *aqua vitae* of the alchemists are parents to this water that is still capable of "rejoicing," that dissolves things with a suspiciously pathetic languor, and that consists of tightly packed "parts." Each of these traits is commonly attributed to water by Newton and his contemporaries and less commonly by contemporary scientists, for whom it is much more congenial to speak of water as a "pure, colorless, transparent, odorless, and almost taste-less liquid," if not simply to describe it by its chemical properties.

"Water" in Newton's passage is beginning to turn into an open gesture toward water. There are here no ethical or sacral intentions. There still remains a vestige of the anthropomorphic, but we can sense how deep is the change from ancient science. The difficult and hesitant development of ancient science can be ex-plained in many ways. One factor was an innate resistance against purging language, which had been brought into being not to assure a free-field for knowing but to create an exit from the bondage of being-in-the-world.

This point can be developed by reference to an eighteenth-century text by Rouhault that offers a *System of Natural Philosophy* (1723) "taken mostly out of Sir Isaac Newton's Philosophy" and that, in fact, reduces a more vivid language to a flaccid and colorless one:

> Now if we examine what (amongst all the Things in Nature) a Mass, consisting of an infinite Number of these small Bodies, which were formed in those *undulating* Pores, like so many Moulds, and which consequently resemble small Threads, which must be very pliable, because during the formation of them, they were several times bent different ways, may be compared to; we shall have reason to think that it exactly resembles what we call Water, and is of the same Nature; because we shall find in it all the Properties which we observe to be in Water.[25]

The barbarous antecedent clause is part of the point—not that the language of scientific account needs to be clumsy but that the attention to water, the pointing outward toward the humanless thing, is achieved here by the elaborate postponement of the object itself. The details of syntax contribute to the same point. They are sensuous enough to stress undulation and the *nematoid*, but that sensuousness does not draw humanized awarenesses out from the element in toward us, rather takes us out toward the element in its full thingliness. The achievement here is a thingliness-in-language, not a passage from language into the thing, not a sensualization for humanely relevant argument. The operations from and into freedom still show themselves in the making of such a passage, as do the psychological factors we discussed previously.

The last passage of early science, from Robert Boyle, suggests the limits of the present point. Boyle's passage will have to stand for the fact that even the most fertile scientific thought can only go so far in "drawing attention to its object." Boyle writes,

> I considered, that the interstellar part of the universe, consisting of air and ether, of fluids analogous to one of them, is diaphanous, and that the ether is as it were, a vast ocean, wherein the luminous globes, that here and there, like fishes, swim by their own motion, or like bodies in whirlpools are carried about by the ambient, are but very thinly dispersed, and consequently that the proportion that the fixed stars and planetary bodies bear to the diaphanous part of the world, is exceedingly small and considerably scarce.[26]

The passage draws attention to its referent, interstellar space, bringing water into supporting and sensuous relation with a scientific assertion as we had earlier, say in Lao Tzu or a passage from the Buddha, seen water brought into relation with ethical assertions. It is not just that the sensuous aquatic vision is ornamenting a more abstract point about cosmic structure. The sensuous here is playing its part in the cognitive thrust of the passage, helping us to know what interstellar space is like. Does this passage show the scientific use of language in the sense defined earlier in this chapter? Are we being brought to question whether there is any special use of language that pertains to scientific argument?

We can look back at a few passages in which "water" was part of an ethical or religious argument. We have seen the "viscosity of the water" surrounding the castle of the Fisher King, and the water in which swimming fish would find freedom of the kind given by the Grail; and at each point the sense qualities of water-experience reinforced an argument and became part of that argument. In that respect "water" was doing there what it is doing in the passage from Boyle. We can make our distinction only on the old grounds: distinguishing between the human-directed references of the "water" in the ethical passages and the object-directed, extraverted reference of the passage from Boyle, as well as in those more obvious cases from Fox, Newton, and Rouhault. The "water" in Boyle's passage leads to states of affairs that belong in the universe-stripped-of-man. This may seem a slight distinction, one affecting the directions rather than the natures of statements, and in a sense it is slight; the nature of things guarantees the existence of thresholds among the major zones of language use. But the slight difference is, in this case, important and, because it seems so easily to hide itself, may, in fact, have been crucial for many centuries in retarding the development of scientific thought. The humanization of language—which leads it naturally into fictions of every kind—lies so close to us that we require natural disaster or the slow ferment of curiosity to lead us into talking about, carefully naming, the physical ambience. A serious change in the direction of statements has in that sense been of vast importance. In a period of four centuries, man has learned how to manipulate his environment, and how to destroy himself. It depends on the direction of statements in language.

My next scientific passages—drawn from the history of biology and limnology—take us back to modes of letting-the-object-be, though now with enough local differences to remind us of the uniqueness even of every scientific statement.

The first passage is from some *Observations* of Leeuwenhoek reporting on those inquiries that led him to the discovery of "animalcules," the first studied specimens of bacteria. We would have trouble imagining a drier account of water in any text destined to find in that element an unexpected source of teeming life.

> May 26th, 1676, it rained very hard; the rain growing less, I caused some of that rain-water running down from a slated roof, to be gathered in a clean glass, after it had been washed two or three times with the water. And in this I observed some few little creatures, and seeing them I thought they might have been produced in the leaden-gutters in some water that might in there have remained before.

And, a little farther on:

> On the same day, the rain continuing, I took a great porcelain dish and exposed it to the free air in my courtyard upon a wooden vessel, about a foot and a half high, so that no earthy parts, from the falling of the rainwater upon that place, might be spattered or dashed into the said dish. With the first water that fell into the dish I washed it (and the glass in which I was

to keep the water) very clean and then flung the water away and received fresh into it, but could discern no living creatures therein.[27]

The first passage recounts the discovery of "little creatures," the second, a further step in experiment, recounts a temporary check in the investigation. We feel that intensity and prudence that mark the first stages of many scientific discoveries. Much scientific language points toward its referent while leaving that referent in itself, there to be studied. With the present passage in which this general point holds, we are able to concentrate on one of the ways in which much scientific observation lets its object alone. At the same time, we note a congruence between such a method and the ethical or religious thought that we have already discovered—as it was negotiating the elements of the free-field established in language.

We are here made to take interest in rain water through *rainwater*. The interest we take is contextual, concerned with free-field making as a way of establishing a new configuration, a syntax in which we can study the names that language calls the world, names that are freshly related and given their meaning by human organization. However, *contextual* seems too passive a term to penetrate the account before us. It is not the case that *water,* say in Leeuwenhoek's *rain-water,* is a nucleus of meaning around which all the other words in its sentence accrete themselves. It is that *I caused some of that* gives something to *rain-water* and takes something from it, as *rain-water* joins naturally in the same negotiation with *roof, glass,* and the other *waters* of the passage. What is negotiatory about such consequences of language is the sense that each word is doing business with the words around it, giving, gaining, trading part of its meaning for part of theirs. A passage like the present shows this operation, concerns and traces a process of discovery that is precisely an enactment of such a negotiation.

My final scientific passage is from Sir Francis Bacon. We see here again—as we did in the passages from Boyle and Leeuwenhoek—what limits scientific language usually imposes on the scientific ideal of leaving-the-object-alone:

It seemeth that fish that are used to the salt water, do nevertheless delight more in fresh. We see, that salmons and smelts love to get into rivers, though it be against the stream. At the haven of Constantinople you shall have great quantities of fish that come from the Euxine Sea, that when they come into the fresh water, do inebriate, and turn up their bellies, so as you may take them with your hand. I doubt there hath not been sufficient experiment made of putting sea-fish into fresh water ponds, and pools. It is a thing of great use and pleasure: for so you may have them new at some good distance from the sea; and besides, it may be, the fish will eat the pleasanter, and may fall to bread. And it is said, that Colchester oysters, which are put into pits, where the sea goeth and cometh, but yet so that there is a fresh water coming also to them when the sea voideth, become by that means fatter, and more grown.[28]

The interest we take in such a passage is like that provoked by the Mandaean passages on pure and turbid water. There deep strata of the inner sense of the aquatic were called on, and for the first time it seemed necessary to introduce the "psychological" account of the experience of water. Bacon might have approved of what we are calling the phenomenological account of such a passage. That account fits perfectly here. What is accounted for is totally and flatly present, semicomically involved with oyster transplanting. Like all good comic-analytic language this raises its referents into a crisp, ikonic freedom, releases the absurd into a state of being attended to. In the previous passage we saw a drama enacted in syntax, though at first pretty plain statements seemed to have been involved. In a passage like Bacon's, we see that kind of drama going on first at a level of psychic syntax. The water itself is left alone. We are asked to view it and what happens in it as it is; and yet we are drawn into the matter verbally by the releasing of our senses of aquatic salinity versus aquatic freshness. This is scientific language, but who would exclude it from a study of the development of English prose style?

Scientific language is a variant on ethical or religious or simply "superstitious" language, as such types of language direct themselves toward a single element of the world they are naming. The scientific variation—coming late on the human scene—involves a new anxiety to leave the object alone, to direct objective attention to it; involves a willingness that runs against the grain of human expression, and is in a way unnatural—as Gaston Bachelard says that scientific thought must be.

From our opening remarks on scientific languages, however, another kind of point has been enforcing itself. It was clear in Newton but became clearer in Boyle, Leeuwenhoek, and finally grew obvious in Bacon: leaving the object alone is a kind of scientific ideal but is only partially possible to language, which is a radically humanized undertaking. We would find more of this objectification, this adoption of a subject-object relation, if we turned to *contemporary* physical science—where the application of mathematical argument to investigation has done a great deal to distance research from the problems of ordinary language. The language of the *development* of modern science was quite naturally of a piece with the language in use for ethical and religious argument in the sixteenth and seventeenth centuries. Threshold formations depend on the historical instant that gives birth to them.

To some extent, the language of early modern science did fight against the human, as a referential component of its statements; and to that extent it achieved in expression what we know was also, gradually and by fits and starts, being achieved in philosophy and religion—the very slow undermining of the perceptual habits that had supported a god-filled universe. Newtonian space was in that sense a product of the same intentions that created Descartes' *méthode,* Spinoza's *Ethics,* and Locke's *Essay on Human Understanding* with its effort to find in primary qualities—space, figure, density—the ultimate structure of the perceived world. It is no surprise to find that the language of the first modern scientists, the organ with which they felt their new world, should have met with the same respondent touch as those new philosophies that were systems of perception established in language.

Poetry's Self-Reference

Three characteristic language-moments have been mentioned. In terms of the element water, I analyzed a few passages from the fifth century before Christ, from the Middle Ages, and from early modern science. The kinds of statements considered were applicable to any kind of subject matter. (Statements are first of all modes—scientific, lyrical, religious, ethical—of negotiation with what-is, and as such they can engage with any material.) But this is not the whole story because subject matter is only partially independent of statements about it. It is apprehended and brought into at least human being by those statements. And those statements are in turn qualified by what they negotiate with—by the matter, ideas, or relationships in question. So, to speak of scientific, religious, or lyrical modes of statement is to speak of distinctive kinds of negotiation we undertake with the world we are humanizing through language. To isolate the nature of the poetic mode peculiarly requires understanding that statements are not defined by context. There is a limited sense—and in the unexamining mind a large sense—in which statements in science, religion, and ethics are about distinctive matters: say about the physical world, the world of spirit, and the realm of the good and the evil. The sense in which any of these points are true is of slight interest. But there is not even a limited sense in which poetic statements are about any distinctive matter. There are no poetic words, poetic thoughts, or even poetic situations. There are simply poetic statements.

First a short poem by Wallace Stevens, "The Glass of Water":

That a glass would melt in heat,
That the water would freeze in cold,
Shows that this object is merely a state,
One of many, between two poles. So,
In the metaphysical, there are these poles.

Here in the centre stands the glass. Light
Is the lion that comes down to drink. There
And in that state, the glass is a pool.
Ruddy are his eyes and ruddy are his claws
When light comes down to wet his frothy jaws.

And in the water winding weeds move round.
And there and in another state—the refractions,
The metaphysica, the plastic parts of poems
Crash in the mind—But, fat Jocundus, worrying
About what stands here in the centre, not the glass,

But in the centre of our lives, this time, this day,
It is a state, this spring among the politicians
Playing cards. In a village of the indigenes,

One would have still to discover. Among the dogs and dung,
One would continue to contend with one's ideas.[29]

There are difficulties of interpretation here; they lie in the transition introduced by *metaphysica* (line 13), out from the first metaphysical state into the only loosely related centrality occupied by the ideas of the last stanza. "Water" is in any case central in the three major situations of the poem. In that sense the poem, while hard, as Stevens always is, is dominantly watery.

Water's centrality depends here on its intermediate status between ice and steam. This status places water in physics and metaphysics and even in fallen human discourse, which turns not around the glass that contains but around the water that is contained. We see the kind of aquatic statement being made and how it is not like those normal in science or religion.

I suppose that *water* (lines 2, 11) is here not less about water than the word had been about the thing in Newton or Boyle. Much of the force of the "being about" in Newton, say, had resulted not from the force of the particular word *water,* but from its syntactical operations. But there is an additional effect of the use of water here that is not to be found in scientific statements. I mean the self-referential dimension in the use of the word *water,* which drives its force back into itself, and into the whole context that the poem has become around it. The first of these points is the clearer and helps to explain the second. The "water" that "would freeze in cold" is impeccably tricked out as the water of a textbook of physics; yet at the same time, it incarnates, as a word, qualities of water that have been totally absorbed into the word. *Water* is in that sense ikonic here.

At this stage another side of the same argument needs airing. I mean the contrast of poetic statement with ethical or religious statement, as it bears on water. We can think back to the discussion between Lao Tzu and Master Meng, where it was a question of interpreting the meanings of the way water flows. From the discussion, Master Meng concluded that "human nature tends toward goodness just as water tends to flow downward." We were only incidentally asked to care what water is in the physical world, or what it does there. Our attention was effectively drawn to "water," and to *water* as a term in analogy for argument's sake. In that drawing of attention there was little interest in an organic relation between the presumed physical action of water and man's ethical life; not even that bond was stressed or dramatized, and the relation between the natural and the ethical was only arbitrarily stressed. The ethical statement takes less interest even than the aesthetic statement in the natural thing-in-itself. But that isn't the only difference between ethical and poetic statement. Like the scientific statement—though in a different direction—the ethical statement moves away from the verbal pointer that anchors the particular ethical argument. The use of water as "water" in ethical, as well as in scientific, statements helps to put into relief the use made of such an element in poetic statement. The *water* in Stevens' poem, unlike the *waters* of Meng Tzu or Newton, is of, and invites interest in, itself as spelled sound.

The structure of the act that brings poetic statements into being is a feeling-structure in just the way suggested here. The "water" in Stevens' poem has become clear, central, or murky with a clarity and syntactically shaped exactitude which water never has for us. The water that we are in the depths of our psyches and that answers to the water in nature is physically cleared, given egress from the caverns and vesicles of memory by the experience of such a poem. The same feeling invites the classic description in terms of the loosening of name from named, the establishing of a new field of perceptual meeting, and self-transcendence through the structured and freshened symbol. Such self-transcendence is the test of this phenomenological account's accuracy; we work peculiarly far out beyond ourselves, becoming what we weren't before, in going through the syntax this poem is. Going through "water" becomes here an unmistakable instance of going through the texture of oneself as language.

Two other water-passages from modern poems, one from Theodore Roethke's "Meditation at Oyster River," the other from T. S. Eliot's *Four Quartets*.

Roethke's poem is a profoundly morbid twilight trance at the side of a river, and in it we see water behaving more obviously within poetic statement than we did in the previous example. In Stevens' passage the problem was to show that the water in its glass was tightly held within itself and within its poem, unlike that scientific water—say, Leeuwenhoek's—which tends urgently toward its external referent. In the present passage that distinction will be self-evident, but the difference between poetic and ethical or religious use of water will require a new kind of attention. The second section runs this way:

> The self persists like a dying star,
> In sleep, afraid. Death's face rises afresh,
> Among the shy beasts, the deer at the salt-lick,
> The doe with its sloped shoulders loping across the highway,
> The young snake, poised in green leaves, waiting for its fly,
> The hummingbird, whirring from quince-blossom to morning-glory—
>
> With those I would be.
> And with water: the waves coming forward, without cessation,
> The waves, altered by sand-bars, beds of kelp, miscellaneous drift-wood,
> Topped by cross-winds, tugged at by sinuous undercurrents
> The tide rustling in, sliding between the ridges of stone.
> The tongues of water, creeping in, quietly.[30]

Here there is no scientific desire to designate water as some thing out there, beyond our feelings, though the sensuous feel of water is in here, in *water* and the entire text, as it had been in some examples of alchemical language. Such presence of the thing, though, is in the present passage drawn up quickly into ethical rhetoric, into a vicarious experience through nature of grave moral considerations the exact nature of which is never determined. In fact, even that "water" is poetic not ethical "water." Look at the *water* of *And with water,* a most quietly declarative phrase.

The *And with water* of this phrase releases a strong affective mood, but that mood remains close to the word that conveys it. It is crucial here that the mood and the conveying word never detach themselves from their own natures. Nor do they detach themselves from the passage in which they are embedded, to enter independent speculations concerning the ethical or religious spheres. This point gains body from contrast with the ethical or religious statements considered earlier. I have referred back to the passage from Master Meng, where "water" is of interest for what its physical movements suggest as a formal analogy to moral argument. We here detach our concern rapidly from "water" and attach it to what we are becoming as reason. This point, in these terms, can be made for many of the earlier ethical arguments: for the first passage from the *Tao te ching*; with qualifications, for the passage from the *Vedanta-Sutras*; for the passage in *The Teaching of Buddha*. In each of those cases, we are made to become a reasoning about ethics after a groundwork of elemental meaning has been laid. In the passage from Roethke, though, we never leave in awareness the language of *water* or of *waves, tongues of water*, or *cross-winds*. When we have done, the argument subsides into itself. The passage and its words have been things in themselves, like musical notes. We can't say that the affective dimension of such experience has no ethical reverberations. But in contrast to the points suggested explicitly by several earlier passages, the present passage closes back onto itself at the end, its ethical dimension proving to be no more than another way of looking at its aesthetic statement. Seeing this is a way of seeing that the statement in poetic language is as subtly separable from the ethical as it is from the scientific statement.

The last passage of poetry will be the opening of "The Dry Salvages" from the *Four Quartets*. It is a piece in which the word *water* will scarcely appear (once only), and there only as a hint toward the wateriness of the entire passage:

> I do not know much about gods; but I think that the river
> Is a strong brown god—sullen, untamed and untractable.
> Patient to some degree, at first recognised as a frontier;
> Useful, untrustworthy, as a conveyor of commerce;
> Then only a problem confronting the builder of bridges.
> The problem once solved, the born god is almost forgotten
> By the dwellers in cities—ever, however, implacable,
> Keeping his seasons and rages, destroyer, reminder
> Of what men choose to forget. Unhonoured, unpropitiated
> By worshippers of the machine, but waiting, watching and waiting.
> His rhythm was present in the nursery bedroom,

In the rank ailanthus of the April dooryard,
In the smell of grapes on the autumn table,
And the evening circle in the winter gaslight.

The river is within us, the sea is all about us;
The Sea is the land's edge also, the granite
Into which it reaches, the beaches where it tosses
Its hints of earlier and other creation:
The starfish, the hermit crab, the whale's backbone;
The pools where it offers to our curiosity
The more delicate algae and the sea anemone.
It tosses up our losses, the torn seine,
The shattered lobsterpot, the broken oar
And the gear of foreign dead men. The sea has many voices,
Many Gods and many voices.
                    The salt is on the briar rose,
The fog is in the fir trees.
          The sea howl
And the sea yelp, are different voices
Often together heard; the whine in the rigging,
The merge and caress of wave that breaks on water,
The distant rot in the granite teeth,
And the wailing warning from the approaching headland
Are all sea voices, and the heaving groaner
Rounded homewards, and the seagull:
And under the oppression of the silent fog
The tolling bell
Measures time not our time, rung by the unhurried
Ground swell, a time
Older than the time of chronometers, older
Than time counted by anxious worried women
Lying awake, calculating the future,
Trying to unweave, unwind, unravel
And piece together the past and the future,
Between midnight and dawn, when the past is all deception,
The future futureless, before the morning watch
When time stops and time is never ending;
And the ground swell, that is and was from the beginning,
Clangs
The bell.[31]

The freeing of "water" from water is apparent, as is our self-transcendence through the product. Even more obvious is the release, through opening out, of some profound inner sense of what water is in us. This second account leads toward what in the statement of Eliot's passage most marks it as poetic. I am thinking of a different way—from that noticed in Stevens or Roethke—in which water can in poetic statement hold itself close in to the text. This different way has to do with the notion of wateriness.

Eliot's whole passage is full of water, through "water" and chiefly through "wateriness." The rhythm of water pervades the lines, which are as waving, sinuous, subsiding, and outpouring as the sea. This miming through sonority, and the extending of sonority over the entire section, creates an effect that is like the effect of the sea itself. In all this, though, there is no trace of a pointing toward the sea, no directionality in the statement. That feature of scientific or ethical statement is lacking. Instead we find another version of the ikonic, self-referential, autonomous character of language in poetic statement. No particular word is crucial, and it matters less than in any passage we have seen that water should be named. What matters is context, "syntax," and above all, the almost hypnotic achievement of language in making what we are become it and nothing else. This language has completely replaced its referents. In transcending ourselves through such language we become a richer density of what we already are.

Fragments of Stevens, Roethke, and Eliot have been considered as poetic statements, and a limited definition of the poetic—established by contrast—has come to the surface. Poetic statements may be composed of the same words, in the same orders as scientific, ethical, or religious statements. We can imagine a sentence like "Water is the most supple element" entering, in appropriate context, into statements in any of those realms. The peculiarity of such utterance in the poetic mode is its ikonic, self-referential character. There it would distinguish itself from other kinds of statements with which poetic statement would, though, finally share its subordination to the structural character of all language making.

I conclude this section with passages of literary prose from James Joyce and René Char. It will be of interest that these passages, too, nearly confuse themselves with other kinds of statement—the Joyce with scientific, the Char with ethical-religious, statements. Poetic-literary statement is uniquely neutral or plastic, on its middle ground lending itself to a variety of intentions that it makes its own only by a kind of reflexive accent.

The passage from Joyce is drawn from the penultimate chapter of *Ulysses,* shortly into the sequence of catechetical questions addressed to Bloom. I quote the entire passage, which gains much of its character from its startling amplitude:

What in water did Bloom, waterlover, drawer of water, water-carrier returning to the range, admire?

Its universality: its democratic equality and constancy to its nature in seeking its own level: its vastness in the ocean of Mercator's projection: its unplumbed profundity in the Sundam trench of the Pacific exceeding 8,000 fathoms: the restlessness of its waves and surface particles visiting in turn all points of its seaboard: the independence of its units: the variability of states of sea: its hydrostatic quiescence in calm: its hydrokinetic turgidity in neap and spring tides: its subsidence after devastation: its sterility in the circumpolar icecaps, arctic and antarctic: its climatic and commercial significance: its preponderance of 3 to 1 over the dry land of the globe: its indisputable hegemony extending in square leagues over all the region below the subequatorial tropic of Capricorn: the multisecular stability of its primeval basin: its luteofulvous bed: its capacity to dissolve and hold in solution all soluble substances including millions of tons of the most precious metals: its slow erosions of peninsulas and downward tending promontories: its alluvial deposits: its weight and volume and density: its imperturbability in lagoons and highland tarns: its gradation of colours in the torrid and temperate and frigid zones: its vehicular ramifications in continental lake contained streams and confluent oceanflowing rivers with their tributaries and transoceanic currents: gulfstream, north and south equatorial courses: its violence in seaquakes, waterspouts, artesian wells, eruptions, torrents, eddies, freshets, spates, groundswells, watersheds, waterpartings, geysers, cataracts, whirlpools, maelstroms, inundations, deluges, cloudbursts: its vast circumterrestrial ahorizontal curve: its secrecy in springs, and latent humidity, revealed by rhabdomantic or hygrometric instruments and exemplified by the hole in the wall at Ashtown gate, saturation of air, distillation of dew: the simplicity of its composition, two constituent parts of hydrogen with one constituent part of oxygen: its healing virtues: its perservering penetrativeness in runnels, gullies, inadequate dams, leaks on shipboard: its properties for cleansing, quenching thirst and fire, nourishing vegetation: its infallibility as paradigm and paragon: its metamorphoses as vapour, mist, cloud, rain, sleet, snow, hail: its strength in rigid hydrants: its variety of forms in loughs and bays and gulfs and bights and guts and lagoons and atolls and archipelagos and sounds

and fjords and minches and tidal estuaries and arms of sea; its solidity in
glaciers, icebergs, icefloes: its docility in working hydraulic millwheels,
turbines, dynamos, electric power stations, bleach works, tanneries, scutch-
mills: its utility in canals, rivers, if navigable, floating and graving docks:
its potentiality derivable from harnessed tides of watercourses falling from
level to level: its submarine fauna and flora (anacoustic, photophobe)
numerically, if not literally, the inhabitants of the globe: its ubiquity as
constituting 90% of the human body: the noxiousness of its effluvia in
lacustrine marshes, pestilential fens, faded flowerwater, stagnant pools in
the waning moon.[32]

It would be hard to imagine a clearer example of the self-
referential in language. Far more than the passages of poetry analyzed above, this one includes statements that could be direct
extracts from scientific texts: "the independence of its units," "its
hydrokinetic turgidity in neap and spring tides," "the multisecular
stability of its primeval basin." Even in these extracts, though,
context alone does not establish the character of the intention. (We
could find poetic passages like that.) Here word groupings like
hydrokinetic turgidity or single words like *multisecular* give away the
ironic tone. So do long lists of technical terms, like those following
"in loughs and bays and gulfs" toward the end of the passage. Such
ironic tone is an inflection, in this language an inner voice, that
invites attention to the language for its own sake.

Again in this case, then, we are seeing language closed in on
itself. But we are also seeing ikonic closure establishing itself within
the larger rhythm of language making. That subordination may
here be especially evident; for in such self-referential language, the
release of word from thing is at its most obvious. What is to man
most uncontrollably other, say about water, has here in "water"
become determinable and stable. Our self-transcendence through
this aesthetic "water" provides an accordingly measurable and intelligible form of being-in-the-world. That kind of move into freedom is in both ethical and religious statements made more turbu-
lent by the fact that their intentions are challenges to self, at the
same time that the statements are vehicles by which the self can
move. Even scientific statements, while not in that sense challenges,
add to the modal complexity of what-is-said, and in doing so
displace some of the directness of self-transcendent thrust through
language. This contrast gives us still another way to gauge the

special character of aesthetic statements. That special character will affect the kinds of psychic freedom and inner syntax that mark such statements.

My last instances of poetic statement are three gnomic utterances from René Char:

> There will always be a drop of water to outlast the sun, without shaking the sun's ascendancy.

> I am eager to hold in my hands the joy of yours. Sometimes I imagine it would be good to drown in a pond where no keel would dare to come. Later, to revive in the current of a real torrent where your colors swirl.

> There are two yellow irises in the green water of the Sorgue. If the current carried them down, it would be because they were beheaded.[33]

Poetic statements like these raise mimetic, and thereby ontological, questions of the relation between the literary work and the world it is "about." Here are strong senses of the way water offers itself to us phenomenally, as a movement with moral charge. We find that sense in the enduring "drop of water," the "pond where no keel would dare to come," the "real torrent," the "green water of the Sorgue." We sense presented water with all its humanized charge just on the other side of the words. What meaning can it have, then, to say that such words are autonomous and self-referential, as words are in poetic language?

The human phenomenon that brings language into the field of experience is a radical novelty in being. With it comes reflective consciousness, closely followed by self-examination geared to what in the largest sense we should call action; and with that gearing is established the possibility of free-fields, those areas of experience that the animal man can dispose in front of him and work through; areas that language is especially apt at keeping open but structured, made out of a certain carefully constructed density from which we can learn by making our way. In making and becoming language, man is in every sense moving out from the phenomena of the given

world—which is of course already partly him, even when given—
toward the unknown, the always-in-process-of-becoming that language is. Understanding this direction inward to language from
the world helps us understand the relation of "water" to the named
waters in Char's passages. The move into language is always new:
in Char's own words, "l'acte est toujours vierge, même répété"
("the act is always virgin, even when repeated").

The passages from Char carry the scent of phenomenal experience on them and seem, more even than scientific passages
whose intentions are the world's *realia,* to strive toward those
realia. It marks the moving-out-from-the-world in scientific language that it should continue to designate things in the world. But
it is not part of the poetic move out—even in this language of
Char—to designate things in the world. An aroma is preserved.
The language itself, however, has even here become dense, self-
enclosed, completely the sense it is about. We see this easily by
comparing the passages from Char with the discussions of water
in Newton and Leeuwenhoek, where language was, as is usually
and properly the case in the arguments of science, without density.

I assumed that being-in-the-world is negotiation and that in
its human form it is a negotiation in which both subject and object
enter as determinants. Language was seen to fit and to confirm this
account of our situation; for language represents a highly complex
and effectual negotiation in which the object is distilled, placed in
new relationships, and proposed by self to itself for transcendence.
Language being the human act par excellence, I found in it a strong
support for the negotiatory account of human being-in-the-world.

These aspects of being-in-the-world and of language are parts
of our total situation, without reference to which a well-grounded
establishment of terminology cannot be understood. In general,
terms like *phenomenological* and *psychological* are ways we add emphasis and pressure to particular areas of our experience. They are
not ways of cutting up the world because they arise out of the
constantly forming and reforming transaction of subject and object,
inner and outer, that self is. Terminology of this sort in question
is a translation of philosophical realism into an existential context.

What about the particular terms worked with? *Phenomenolog-ical* and *psychological* arise in the course of our work with the world, as beings who are in that world and whom that world is. "Phe-nomenological" analysis is taking place at the point where we turn in on the bare existential structure we are, in the act of making language. That in-turning is the most nearly essential perception possible to us. "Psychological" analysis added itself to "phenome-nological" by the natural prompting of the argument and first took place in connection with Mandaean texts of which it rapidly became necessary to discuss the subterranean sources. Saying what ap-peared to be happening there seemed to involve reading a key-language, a *langue à clef*; and the term *psychological* went before us like a banner. *Psychological* was another way of saying *phenomeno-logical,* and the use of those two terms involved doing essentially the same work. Neither of these terms was applied to substantive states of affairs, but only to dynamic states that were naturally ways in which matters of substance transpired.

Particular kinds of statement are matters of substance tran-spiring in those dynamic ways that psychological and phenome-nological accounts are designed to name. Reflection on the kinds of statement considered earlier—say in Lao Tzu, the Buddha, Newton, or Stevens—suggests in what sense matters of substance are here to be considered dynamic. These matters are statements in the process of transpiring. They are moving substances to the contours of which accounts, phenomenological or psychological, attempt to hew.

The implication of the outer in language, from the inception of language in the human creator, complicates efforts to carry further the discussion of the kinds of work done by ethical, aes-thetic, and scientific statements. But we need to grasp these state-ments at the sense in which they are full of the world and thus occur in and toward the "outward." If we are being-in-the-world, it follows that our language is in some sense always a presence in that world.

From whichever broader account they are viewed, aesthetic statements are normative in the (surprising) sense that they arrest the directionality inherent in units of language. That directionality is what appears in scientific and religious or ethical statements to tend toward an area of experience—the world of the other in nature or the world of the self—which does not have its centers in language or in the particular language-work in question. Such directionality is not entirely absent from aesthetic statements: it is, for instance, present in passages from Joyce, Roethke, and Stevens. However, the chief pressure of language, even in those three instances, is in onto itself. We are made to go out to the texts but not far beyond them and not beyond them for long. This is the normative situation of aesthetic statements, a situation clear enough under analysis as a sequence of phenomena; of freeing of word from world, of establishment of a free syntactical field, then of transcendence into and through the structure; a pattern worked out with greatest exactitude by aesthetic statements in which expressed awarenesses are held, retained as it were, in storage for transactions. Such statements are uniquely fitted for us to enter, go through, and emerge with on their far side.

Normative cannot be further explained. Aesthetic statement certainly does not "give the rule" to statements of other kinds. It does not precede them or make history before them. Because of its ikonic and arrested force, however, aesthetic statement helps us to see how other events in language disperse themselves. It helps make visible those thresholds in difference that lead in and out of language's several houses.

Such a view of the aesthetic should help us when it comes to the cognitive function of statements. I earlier mentioned the unique "arrested intentions" of aesthetic statements, their disjunction from intentions and ends. I tried to break down any static dualism of subject and object in the work of language and to see language—whether scientific or aesthetic—as a way in which something extrapersonal and extraobjective comes into being. In many respects the aesthetic intention is not unlike other intentions in language. Finally the aesthetic shares with all other statements in language a quality of being-there-to-be-transcended. The human ground is finally the determinant in this respect. This self-transcendence, which we achieve at least through all significant language, occurs regardless of the intentional force of particular kinds of statement. Self-transcendence is our way of coming through on the other side of our language, whether that language takes us back into things, into ourselves, or into ikonic units of itself.

The Quanta of Imagination

You ask me how a *portent* can possibly be wound in a *shell*. Without attempting to answer this for the moment, I ask you how Blake could possibly say that *"a sigh is a sword of an Angel King."*

Hart Crane

In their artistic creativity the Greeks went far beyond their theory. Plato's own imaginative vision—which went beyond his aesthetics—is a perfect example, making us wonder how the imaginer of the cave could so easily be stopped by the problem of artifice, by the conundrum of those sense deceptions on which great artists routinely depend.

This plight of conceptual theory is baffling throughout classical antiquity. Aristotle speaks about *phantasia* as that which provides the schemata of thought. He was trying to give an account of mental faculties and to support powerful distinctions—among, for instance, imagination, sensation, and thinking; but he was in fact just leaving open, to the long tradition that was to follow him, a welcome chance to view the imagination as what Hobbes later called *fancy,* "a decaying sense," a mental operation corruptly material. Throughout that long tradition—from Aristotle to the eighteenth century—runs the underlying notion that imagination is essentially visual, image making, and, in that capacity, wrapped up in delusion, unequipped to distinguish truth from falsehood.

What way out was there between the visionary perspective onto *phantasia* (found in the *Timaeus*) and the view of imagination as twin sister to fancy, wit, and other mechanical or otherwise dubious operations—that view dominant in early post-Renaissance literary theory? The way out had to pass through the shadow of critical death, a reduction of the whole question to basic terms—Locke's and Addison's—on which, slowly, the Romantic wisdom of metaphor could be erected. Locke scrubs the mind clean of all shadows and looks into it, watching the way it constructs a world out of the rudiments of experience. Our sense perceptions and our reflections onto them are the primary operations by which our world enters us. By any reflection onto our reflections, however, we become aware of the speed with which we leave the ground of experience. Locke believes that the primary qualities of the world—size, shape, weight—are part of the ground; but that secondary qualities—color, taste, smell—are already off the ground, away from the ground, mind-plus-the-ground. As soon as he leaves the ground, Locke is faced with the "workmanship" of the mind. That workmanship is to him typically reflected in memory, comparison, consciousness of pleasure and pain. But though he has little interest in aesthetic questions, even as they were imposed on him by the terms of his time, he contributes most to them by setting their stage and naming the moment when they appear; when "workmanship" begins.

Addison's theory—say in *The Pleasures of the Imagination* (1711)—aids the construction of a richer aesthetic, as basically anti-imaginative theories are often able to do. He is at times a meat-and-potatoes Locke: art does not have the capacity to improve on nature; imagination, the chief factor in art, is a recording visual faculty through which, in its primary form, we are struck by a seen object and through which, in its secondary form, we cull in our memories "visions of things that are either absent or fictitious" (*Spectator* no. 411). In the same argument he maintains—as though translating Locke's theory to his own account—that pleasures of imagination are not as great as those of understanding, because they add nothing new to mind. Only "charms," he says, are added through pleasures of imagination.

Like most critics of his time, Addison is especially interested in true wit, which combines potentially congruous ideas, while false wit is content with surface—bringing together congruous words, syllables, sometimes (in concrete poetry) even letters. The truer the wit, the better. True or false, though, the operation of this faculty has some resemblance to Coleridge's *imagination*. Addison took little interest in the cognitive relation of wit to the knowable world; if he had, he would have entered the philosophical problem-context in which Coleridge placed literary creativity.

In chapter 13 of *Biographia Literaria* Coleridge distinguishes between fancy and imagination. The distinction is not new. New is the copiousness of the definition of imagination and the energy with which numerous categories (*phantasia,* wit, decaying sense) are herded into the pen of fancy. "*Fancy* . . . has no other counters to play with but fixities and definites." The process will not fuse with its objects, themselves already borrowed from the outer world: "The Fancy is indeed no other than a mode of Memory emancipated from the order of time and space; while it is blended with, and modified by that empirical phenomenon of the will, which we express by the word CHOICE." Imagination differs from fancy in its imitation of an eternal act, in its struggling power, and in its destiny to dissolve and then to recreate, whereas fancy does not change the nature of, but only juxtaposes, the elements of what it acts on.

"The IMAGINATION, then, I consider either as primary, or secondary. The primary IMAGINATION I hold to be the living Power and prime Agent of all human Perception, and as a repetition in the finite mind of the eternal act of creation in the infinite I AM." The genuine art-making work, which operates through secondary imagination, is fully meaningful *only* as part of that life force which the primary imagination is: "The secondary [IMAGINATION] I consider as an echo of the former, co-existing with the conscious will, yet still as identical with the primary in the *kind* of its agency, and differing only in *degree,* and in the *mode* of its operation." The secondary imagination "dissolves, diffuses, dissipates, in order to re-create; or where this process is rendered impossible, yet still at all events it struggles to idealize and to unify." We need a direct object for the verbs "dissolves, diffuses, dissipates," but whatever exactly that outer material is, it is being integrated into a second world. The essential relation between this operation and making a second world is also the reason why the secondary imagination is "essentially *vital,* even as all objects (*as* objects) are essentially fixed

and dead." This is not to say that the imagination does not transform what are best called *objects;* certainly objects are the chief
ingredients of what secondary imagination "dissolves, diffuses,
dissipates, in order to re-create." But those objects are no longer
properly such by the time secondary imagination touches them.
By contrast, the "fixities and definites" of fancy remain—seem
to remain, at least—objectlike even within the fancy and its
works.

I want to work with Coleridge's account of secondary imagination; bring into relation with it some comparable thoughts from
twentieth-century positivism or language analysis, selections that
conflict with, rub against, and enrich Coleridge's aesthetic. This
working with and loosening up belongs to the spirit of the present
book, which tries out new thresholds and relationships. My first
two essays reflected a desire to write down the discovered rather
than to discover the new. To some degree I want to consider this
book an offering of truth, of the way things are. (While there is an
element of fiction at work here—rooted, to start with, in the
metaphor—that element is more nearly a necessary condition than
a chosen form). Yet at the same time, there is here much trying on
for size, much crossing of thresholds by seeing whether they can
be crossed. This experimental element underlies my testing and
enriching of Coleridge's account. I look in the end toward a new
sense of the value and enlargeability of Coleridge's thought and of
our own toward a new threshold crossing at which Romantic
imagination and some perspectives of our century lend new insights
to one another.

Gilbert Ryle's *The Concept of Mind*[1] presents an *imagination*
that seems to imply every conceivable opposition to Coleridge.
(Mile-high thresholds rise, it seems, between the two perspectives.)
The clash is so impressive that at first we believe Ryle and Coleridge
are talking of totally different matters, with similar terms. This is
to some extent the case. Ryle is carefully not referring back into
the aesthetic tradition, culture-laden and hyperconnotative; for he

is interested in analyzing ordinary statements from which we can become clearer about the world we negotiate in. When he discusses imagination, he illustrates by a wide range of inner picturing activities, to which he draws attention by considering the various ways we talk about them. The acerbity of this method clashes sharply with Coleridge.

Ryle draws an analogy about "the University" that illustrates his procedure. A foreign visitor has asked to be shown the University. We take him to see various buildings and at the end of the tour he asks us, "Now can I see the University?" In asking this, he has made what Ryle calls a category mistake, has taken the University to be of the same category as its component parts. In this way he has created a fiction, the University, which is nowhere and nothing—except an abstraction created in that way. Ryle makes the same attack against the concept of mind. We construct that concept, he says, by adding it to many other items that we take to be the activities of mind. To thinking, feeling, remembering, hoping, imagining, we add the concept of mind. However, that concept is nothing more than the activities that go on in it. To consider mind an independent concept is to invite many "systematically misleading concepts" as well as to commit a category mistake. It is hard to see a synthetic view of imagination from an atomistic perspective of this stripe.

Concern with daily language usage promotes Ryle's account of mind, and is the probe by which he fingers his way toward the imagination—which he introduces as *imaging*. He finds that there is a coherent group of activities—reflected in telling expressions— that we can call *imaging*. Examples can be drawn from all sides: from humming half-remembered tunes, "seeing" in ourselves mountains we once saw in fact, picturing our nursery, even from sparring (as distinct from boxing). The range of imaging- (or imagining-) usages is wide, not specifically verbal at all, and not necessarily limited to art: "There is no special Faculty of Imagination, occupying itself singlemindedly in fancied viewings and hearing. On the contrary, 'seeing things' is one exercise of imagination, growling somewhat like a bear is another; smelling things in the mind's nose is an uncommon act of fancy, malingering is a very common one, and so forth."[2] If this seems to put us far from poetic imagination, that is partly due to our assumptions about what is poetic.

Nonetheless, we face a brutal contrast between Coleridge's and Ryle's notions of the mind's central shaping faculty. Nothing is wrong with brutality in its place, but here it is misleading. It hides true and productive affinity between Coleridge and Ryle. We can narrow the distance between their two positions by looking closely at the latter's examples of imagining ourselves in our nursery or of sparring.

Ryle wraps himself in the intricate: "True, a person picturing his nursery is, in a certain way, like that person seeing his nursery, but the similarity does not consist in his really looking at a real likeness of his nursery, but in his really seeming to see his nursery itself, when he is not really seeing it. He is not being a spectator of a resemblance of his nursery, but he is resembling a spectator of his nursery."[3] Imaging is in all imagination a distancing from the thing imaged or imagined. The thing is not present in the imaging as an image of itself but only as such an image-being-experienced-by-us-as-spectators-of-it. Ryle usually includes in this definition the insistence that we are at the same time aware of our participation in the imaging act as spectators. He always insists, though, that such imaging operations are transitive. There is always a source and object of the image. This is one way in which Ryle—like Coleridge—insists on the public dimension of imaging.

The imager's consciousness is more obvious in the example of sparring:

> Let us consider the case of the boxer sparring with his instructor. They go through the motions of serious fighting, though they are not fighting seriously; they pretend to attack, retreat, punish and retaliate, though no victory is aimed at, or defeat feared. The pupil is learning manoeuvres by playing at them, the instructor is teaching them by playing at them. Yet though they are only mock-fighting, they need not be carrying on two collateral activities. They need not be both punching and also pulling their punches. . . . They may be going through only one set of movements, yet they are making these movements in a hypothetical and not in a categorical manner.[4]

In addition to the sparrer's (or hummer's or daydreamer's) consciousness, there is once again a transitive thrust. There is an object. Sparring is indeed the intention of fighting.

Imaging is of a higher order than whatever in the world it is transitive toward, is at least both secondary to and more sophisticated than what is imaged. This is a point to which Ryle returns: "Picturing Helvellyn, so far from having, or being akin to having, visual sensations, is compatible with having no such sensations and nothing akin to them. There is nothing akin to sensations. Realizing, in this way, how Helvellyn would look is doing something which stands in the same relation to seeing Helvellyn as sophisticated performances stand to those more naive performances, whose mention is obliquely contained in the description of the higher order of performances."[5] Ryle's chapter, "Sensation and Observation," lays the ground for this assertion that sensation is like nothing else. Realizing how radically sensation differs from observation helps us see how little *will*—how little of anything voluntary— there is in sensation. And seeing this helps us to appreciate the difference of imaging from directly—or, as Ryle says, "ingenuously"—experiencing. In fact "sophisticated performance," as described in the Helvellyn example, has a connection with the conscious will that brings us back again to Coleridge's definition of imagination. We can now guess that Ryle's element of self-conscious involvement, even of put-on, may have been in Coleridge's intention when he described the relation between secondary imagination and the conscious will with which it "co-exists."

A final clue to Ryle's range:

> Certainly not all imaging is the picturing of real faces and mountains or the "hearing" of familiar tunes and known voices. We can fancy ourselves looking at fabulous mountains. Composers, presumably, can fancy themselves listening to tunes that have never yet been played. It may be supposed, accordingly, that in such cases there is no question of the imaginary scene being pictured right, or of the tune still under composition being "heard" to go otherwise than as it really goes; any more than Hans Andersen could be either accused of misreporting the careers of his characters, or praised for the factual fidelity of his narratives.[6]

It is possible to image what has no external existence, what is already part of our imaging power; for instance, a "fabulous mountain." We are told nothing about the existence status of such objects because Ryle's concern with our manners of formulation manages to cloak that question. But he gives us no reason to think that he scorns music for any false presumption, founding itself upon nothing; and in fact he appreciates that, in music as presentation, which most frees music into the risk of its own inner argument.

I opened this section with certain implications of relating Ryle to Coleridge, of trying to think our ways across the threshold between them. Ryle seemed at first not to be discussing the same imagination as Coleridge. Furthermore he seemed to be dismissing that concept of mind by which Coleridge was able to posit and define imagination.

The workmanship of the mind, as Ryle sees it, is not the product of one great faculty. Like sensation, the mind is what it is. There is nothing like it. Each individual activity of mind is only itself, not the component of a concept. Standing at this point, Ryle casts a dark glance at Coleridge's *faculty of imagination,* and at the whole faculty-psychology traditional for Coleridge and still common. But that is only the surface. That is the condition of threshold as barrier.

In bringing Coleridge and Ryle together on the question of imagination—as I began to do—I argued from a standpoint outside Ryle yet comprehended by Coleridge. I found in Coleridge's view of imagination a certain immunity from the kind of language analysis that concentrates on category mistakes. Coleridge enters that discussion at a more general level of organization than the level on which Ryle attacks. But to value Coleridge, we must anticipate Ryle's assertion that concepts like imagination are reducible to activities like picturing or imaging. The most stimulating defense against Ryle's threat will be to claim an ontological priority for Gestalt concepts over the piecemeal construction of experience that is posited by ordinary language analysis. But in this defense the point is not really to counterattack. It is to use. We are interested here in what Ryle lets Coleridge learn to do, toward formulation of his ideas, toward posthumous self-clarification.

My argument-purpose, to repeat, is to bring Ryle to bear on

Coleridge, to help each cross the threshold between them. Ryle argues a relation between conscious volition and imagination, which resembles Coleridge's argument. In addition, Ryle adopts the related position that make-believe—of the kind he defines—is "of a higher order than . . . belief." "Make-believe" has at least that advantage over ingenuous belief, that it is distanced from its objects. There is, in the final passage from Ryle, the suggestion that in imaging to ourselves what is already only "never played music," we are carrying on work that is properly mind's. It is interesting to remember again the reason why Ryle will not say more, here, about the nature of this work. Ordinary language provides no clue to that nature. Coleridge had no hesitation in attributing that work that is properly mind's, to the dissolving and rejoining capacity of mind.

Max Black's essay on metaphor in *Philosophy Looks at the Arts*[7] helps us to see a direction in which Ryle's description of imagination might naturally flow, if it were to move into one of its own possibilities for aesthetics. (That *if it were* is crucial here, as I am creating an anthology of possibilities, establishing hypotheses and measuring thresholds. I am concerned with what might grow from what and into what. Derrida's *Glas*, an irresponsibly fascinating contemporary collage, simply juxtaposes texts and looks for startling combinations among them. I am looking for juxtapositions that grow into grafts.) Like Ryle, Black proceeds by careful analysis of instances, with healthy distrust both of empty language and of the organic. He arrives at a view of what metaphor is and can do, which seems to take us as far as the underlying position—Ryle's or his own—will permit. He is an excellent test-instance for the kind of rapprochement with Coleridge that concerns me here.

Black first distinguishes between two accounts of metaphor— the substitution and the comparison accounts—that see no substantial changes effected by the metaphorical process, that see metaphors primarily as a source of pleasure and secondarily as an aid to thought. The expression, "Richard is a lion," suggests, according to the substitution account, that the author substitutes something for something else, *a lion* for *brave:* "It is the reader's task to invert the substitution, by using the literal meaning"—of *lion*—"as a clue to the intended literal meaning"—of courageous. "Understanding a metaphor is like deciphering a code or unravelling a riddle." By the comparison account, Richard is actually *like* a lion in some respect; the point made about Richard by the metaphor is strengthened by the bond of courage which joins Richard to a real lion (it mattering, in this regard, not what lions are in fact but what they are in our language use). At this point in exposition, Black has only hinted at his third account of metaphor: "It would be more illuminating in some of these cases to say that metaphor *creates* the similarity than to say that it formulates some similarity antecedently existing."[8] Thus the introduction of *a lion,* in the expression before us, makes a fresh relation between Richard and a lion; a relation already latent in our language habits but in other realms of experience totally unprepared for. This creation is still limited to establishing a code name for the metaphor base, Richard. The third account of metaphor takes into consideration that something has been left out of the first two accounts, the effect of the ground term on the metaphor word, of *Richard* on *a lion.* This effect is accounted for by the interaction theory. The illustrative example is "The poor are the negroes of Europe." *The negroes* here qualifies *the poor* in the way *a lion* qualified *Richard,* although a good deal more richly, as *negroes* is a connotative word of which we are not sure which meanings to isolate here. But *the poor* also qualifies *the negroes,* by specifying the traits of Negroes that are to be emphasized. (And yet the specification is imprecise, for within poverty there are many possible forms of existence, and so on.) *The negroes,* introduced here to qualify *the poor,* is itself qualified. This mutual qualification is what the most Coleridgean of the three accounts, the interaction theory, sees in metaphor. It finds that even the ground and the metaphor terms filter each other; the needed sense of both *the negroes* and *the poor* being filtered out from the extraneous, but still peripherally operative, senses. Understood this way, Black believes, metaphor can be seen as a distinct cognitive vehicle that is useful to thought: "No doubt metaphors are dangerous—and perhaps especially so in philosophy, but a prohibition against their use would be a wilful and harmful restriction upon our power of inquiry."[9]

Analysis of examples, with a sharp eye to what they really say, leads Black to a position that, though friendly to metaphor, and in fact friendly to the notion of metaphor as cognition, is still implicitly hostile to any form of verbal imagination of which we might want to say, that it "dissolves, diffuses, dissipates, in order to re-create." We are still far from making Coleridge and Black sit down together, although the interaction theory of metaphor, positing a mutual fusion of ground and metaphor term within the figure of speech, is a step toward a Romantic account—and a gesture drawing that Romantic account toward it.

That imagination which Ryle describes in its sophisticated higher-order activities would not only be a fitting, but would be *the appropriate*, organ for making Black's interactive metaphor. The actions constituting imaging power—according to Ryle—involve both engagement and removal of the creating self—plus a nonrepresentative representation of whatever is imaged. There is nothing in the imaging itself that would prevent it from joining terms in the interactive richness of metaphor, and in fact that kind of joining would follow as a natural aspect of Ryle's higher-order activities. Yet there is no point in those activities from which we could anticipate dissolution and recreation of the Coleridgean kind. The *essentially* atomistic and mechanical operation for which Black takes the imagination has a natural source in the essentially accumulative, serial operation in which Ryle sees the work of imaging.

Wheelwright (in *Metaphor and Reality*)[10] is sympathetic to poetic discourse as a valid complement to the scientific accounting for the world and tries to keep both types of discourse in harmony. He is sensitive to the value of plurisignative combinations, such as those founded by all kinds of metaphor, and is especially moved by the great metaphors, those symbols—cross, dying god, suffering hero—that mobilize the perceptions and self-definitions of entire cultures. In this anthropological concern he both carries a Romantic aesthetic far into the social and shows his kinship with the analysts of language, working from efforts to define metaphor by its components.

Wheelwright's ontology aids him to intermediate between

Coleridge's vision and that of the analysts. "The nature of reality," he says, "is intrinsically and ultimately hidden from any finite exploration. . . . Reality is ultimately problematical, not contingently so; for to grasp and formulate it, even as a set of questions, is to fragmentize it. There is always, in any inquiry, something more than meets the eye, even the inner eye; the permanent possibility of extending one's imaginative awareness has no limits."[11] Against this background the dissipation and recreation of received experience, the self-affirmed establishment of new reality in language, the language of poetry—all these factors in Coleridge's theory of imagination—become functional and find their place. They acquire a usefulness that they could, of course, never fully enjoy in the (implied) ontology of Ryle or of Black. As we work toward the opening of two traditions to one another we find Wheelwright's whole position helpfully mediate, Janus-headedly sensitive to both the analytical and the Romantic accounts of mind.

Wheelwright establishes a frame in which to set a cognitive theory of metaphor, showing us that for metaphor to serve as a cognitive tool—which even Black believes it does—it must exist in a world in which it could play a useful role. In the discussion of *epiphor* and *diaphor* Wheelwright moves on that level where Black operates in discussing interactive metaphor. There, if anywhere, the positive-pragmatic and the spiritually monist traditions come together, intermingle as though through some hidden pineal gland.

Epiphor, as Wheelwright absorbs the word from Aristotle, "starts by assuming a usual meaning for a word; it then applies this word to something else on the basis of, and in order to indicate, a comparison with what is familiar. The semantic 'movement' (*phora*) here is characteristically from a more concrete and readily graspable image 'over on to' (*epi*) what is perhaps vaguer, more problematic, or more strange."[12] "Life is a dream" is an example; so are "God the Father" and "milk of human kindness." The *epiphor* is the kind of metaphor accounted for by Black under the comparison theory. *Diaphor* is " 'movement' (*phora*) 'through' (*dia*) certain particulars of experience (actual or imagined) in a fresh way, producing new meaning by juxtaposition alone."[13] An example is Ezra Pound's

The apparition of these faces in the crowd;
Petals on a wet black bough.

The element of juxtaposition, which was also important in *epiphor*, is central in *diaphor*.

The *epiphor* is close to that metaphor for which Black thought the comparison account appropriate. *Diaphor* is close to what Black's interaction account explains. There is a filtering interaction, for example, between the "faces" and the "petals" in Pound's couplet. Wheelwright's account, in other words, can be pulled back toward Black's, which—as we saw—is one direction in which Ryle's description of imagination flows. A continuum is momentarily visible, between Ryle and Coleridge—passing through Black and Wheelwright.

The tradition from which Ryle and Black move has some of its roots in the philosophy of Ludwig Wittgenstein. There is no better point at which to deepen our sense of the issues involved in this chapter or of the eclectic possibilities inherent in it. It is not that Wittgenstein helps us see Ryle and Black doing business with Coleridge and Wheelwright in a way we had earlier overlooked. From the Ryle-Black direction, he will help us to reformulate the idea of imagination, to see the continued incorporation of the Romantic in later thought.

In the *Tractatus*[14] Wittgenstein argues a special identity between language and the world. "The world," he says, "is the totality of facts" (1.1). It is not the totality of things or objects; for they are subcomponents of states of affairs, the existence of which constitutes the fact. The world is the totality of "states of affairs," and "it is essential to things that they should be positive constituents of states of affairs" (2.011).

The whole composed in this way proves to be pervaded by logic, as we see what is involved in the composition of states of affairs from things: "If a thing *can* occur in a state of affairs, the possibility of the state of affairs must be written into the thing itself" (2.012) or "If I know an object I also know all its possible occurrences in states of affairs. (Every one of these possibilities must be part of the nature of the object.)" (2.0123) or finally, "If all objects are given, then at the same time all *possible* states of affairs are also given" (2.0124).

At this point in the argument we are dealing with that intelligible network in which the things in the world exist and, in that sense, assume their form. "The possibility of its occurring in states of affairs is the form of an object" (2.0141).

The logic pervading the totality of states of affairs acquires part of its existence from possibility, which itself rests on a necessity: that objects, which make up facts, are what they are and not something else. Since the world has a substance, the sense that propositions make can and must depend on the accuracy with which they are signified. If the world had no such substance, it would not support logic. It would also lack the characteristic of being there to be reproduced, to be accounted for: "In that case we could not sketch out any picture of the world (true or false)" (2.0212). The making of a picture (*Bild*)—and here we come to our issue—of the world is the possibility of representing the logical structure of the world.

"We picture facts to ourselves," we make a *Bild*—a picture— of the *Tatsache,* the fact of which we know that it is a part of that totality which the world is:

> In a picture objects have the elements of the picture corresponding to them. (2.13)

> In a picture the elements of the picture are the representatives of objects. (2.131)

"A picture is a fact" (2.141), therefore, but a fact that represents other facts. Within this kind of picture there is a pervasive form that "resembles" the logic-related form in states of affairs:

> Pictorial form is the possibility that things are related to one another in the same way as the elements of the picture. (2.151)

The picture is "laid against reality like a measure." For this picturing relationship to be possible, there "must be something identical in a picture and what it depicts" (2.161): "A picture can depict any reality whose form it has" (2.171).

The present account of the world and of the picturing activity by which—while being inside the world—we still in a sense know the world contains an additional description of the conditions of the picturing. From this description we can see the themes of "reality" and the imagination clearly emerging:

A picture cannot . . . depict [*abbilden*] its pictorial form: it displays it [*es weist sie auf*]. (2.172)

A picture cannot include an account of what it is as a picture but can only *be* a picture:

A picture represents its subject from a position outside it. (Its standpoint is its representational form.) That is why a picture represents its subject correctly or incorrectly. (2.173)

In order to be able to depict reality correctly or incorrectly, a picture must have a logical form in common with depicted reality. What is the meaning of "correct" or "incorrect" depiction? It seems that a picture can have a logical form identical with that of reality yet can also be incorrect—or correct. The two operations are separate. The question of *being real* is distinct from that of *being correct*. Art's transformatory potency is implied here.

Being real means "being possible," but in a special sense; for instance, "the possibility of all situations" (2.014) is contained in objects, so that we can say of that possibility that it is by no means unanchored contingency; or, since our knowledge of an object is knowledge of "all its possible occurrences in states of affairs" (2.0123), it follows that possibility is grounded in the substantially intelligible. However, *being real* can also mean *being incorrect* or, in that sense, *being about the impossible*. If a picture's reality depicts the impossible, it may still enter the nexus of logical relationships which bind states of affairs. This helps us understand the meaning of *reality* in the following proposition:

A picture depicts reality by representing a possibility of existence and nonexistence of states of affairs. (2.201)

What about *being correct* as distinct from *being real*? How is it possible to depict reality through pictorial form and yet to do so incorrectly, a situation envisaged by 2.17:

> A picture represents its subject from a position outside it. (Its standpoint is its representational form.) That is why a picture represents its subject correctly or incorrectly. (2.173)

We might at first suppose that the inherence of possibility in reality would make incorrectness—and thus also correctness—of depiction an impossibility. But obviously not:

> What a picture must have in common with reality, in order to depict it— correctly or incorrectly—in the way it does, is its pictorial form. (2.17)

Stenius agrees that the pictorial form in question "is determined by some kind of *similarity* between the picture and its prototype that exists *independently* of the truth or falsehood of the picture"; and goes on to suggest that "this means that such a similarity cannot have any reference to the external structure of the fields concerned, but must be a characteristic which can be stated, if at all, simply on an examination of the internal properties of the element and the key of interpretation."[15] *Tractatus* 2.171 seems to comment on this point:

> A picture can depict any reality whose form it has. A spatial picture can depict anything spatial, a colored one anything colored, etc.

Pictorial form can be "adequate" in just this sense, without necessarily depicting the truth.

For any account of imagination there is much to be learned from the *Tractatus*. The picture theory reminds me of Ryle's notion of picturing—and in that way takes us back to our earlier questions. For Wittgenstein even more sharply than for Ryle, "picturing" is not an introduction of the new by way of creative recombinations. (In this regard he remains on the other side of the threshold from Coleridge.) Yet at just this point, Wittgenstein writes into his account of picturing a remarkable possibility for creative picturing. Here his intent and direction differ totally from Ryle's, though we should remember how carefully Ryle accounted for certain asymmetries and higher-order operations that, while resting on no transformation of the world, still seemed to rework the material of the world.

Wittgenstein's separation of correctness and incorrectness—

the *richtig* and the *falsch*—from reality, as objects of picturing, prepares the way for an account of what is real but false; lays the ground for that kind of theory of imagination. It is important to see that the incorrect or false here is not the possible, for possibility inheres in objects and states of affairs in the world. (The incorrect and correct derive from another possibility—itself included within the larger one that the world is—from the possibility of internal isomorphic relationships between the picture and its object.) In positing those relationships Wittgenstein posits the possibility of a new freedom for picturing mind, a freedom from the suffocating plenum in which the real and the true are equated and all valid picturing, perception, or knowing is confined to the accurate representation of reality and truth. Positivism—in Comte and Carnap—often tries on the chains of that plenum world account. But the wide tradition of language analysis provides many examples of the kind of counterargument found here in the *Tractatus*. We come soon to the examples of Frege's *sense* and Russell's negative facts—which have close kinship to Wittgenstein's false depictions of reality and which suggest that positivism contains the germ of its reversal into an imaginative aesthetic. Coleridge himself shows us how willing certain language analysts can be to transcend their own assumptions.

It will hold Wittgenstein's point if we look ahead to a few comments made deeper into the *Tractatus*, especially 4.061 and 4.0621: "It must not be overlooked that a proposition has a sense that is independent of the facts: otherwise one can easily suppose that true and false are relations of equal status between signs and what they signify" (4.061). Wittgenstein does not contradict—but simply refines—the idea that a proposition can be both real and false. The proposition is still invariably a picture of reality: "It can be true or false only in virtue of being a picture of reality" (4.106). Yet the false proposition differs from the true in the relation to reality which it establishes. What is that difference?

The difference is *not* that the false proposition refers to something different in reality from what the true proposition refers to: "It is important that the signs 'p' and '–p' *can* say the same thing. For it shows that nothing in reality corresponds to the sign '–' " (4.0621). This means, as Black says, "simply that the negation sign is not a *name*—that negation is not an object." What is negation?

It is the expression of a sense opposite to that expressed in a given true proposition.

In 4.062 Wittgenstein writes, "Can we not make ourselves understood with false propositions, just as we have done up to now with true ones?—So long as it is known that they are meant to be false.—No! For a proposition is true if we use it to say that things stand in a certain way, and they do; and if by 'p' we mean '–p' and things stand as we mean that they do, then, construed in the new way, 'p' is true and not false" (4.062). Even on the account of falsity that we get in 4.0621 we cannot say that 'p' is false here. For the meaning (the *Sinn*, or "sense") of falseness is given by the intention of the proposition, and the intention of the present proposition confers its truth on it. The "negative fact" appeared to me a promising (and provocative) model of the work of art. I mean that the artwork seems to be both real and false (a peculiarity of interest to Aristotle; when he says that in poetry "a credible impossibility is to be chosen before an incredible possibility" [*Poetics* 61b9], he is defending falseness to fact within reality of reference to a possible state of affairs). In 4.062 Wittgenstein offers an even more promising model for an aesthetic. The negative statement, which presents a false state of affairs, is understood by its speaker to mean the opposite of what it says. By "the book is not on the table" he means "the book is on the table." He uses a negative for a positive proposition. The artwork can be usefully compared to this kind of statement. We can say that the artwork is not simply false by being real but that it makes a negative proposition which it wishes to have understood as positive—and is at the same time real. From within a worldview as noncommittal as Ryle's, Wittgenstein has found his way to a profound grasp both of aesthetic imitation and aesthetic transformation.

Time for a break.

Jacques Derrida's *Glas*[16] is one contemporary work that has readied us to hear texts talking to one another. We are, in his work, not sure why those texts say what they do to one another, but we sharpen our hearing and free our associations by listening to them. His irresponsible collage is creative and provocative.

My present essay shares with, and splits from, Derrida's strategy. I am opening critical texts outward into the bloodstream of Coleridge's aesthetic. This violation of textual autonomy is one grounding principle of my book, as it is of Derrida's. Unlike Derrida I look toward a telos into which to let my opened text-veins flow. The vein just opened—a distinction between the true and the real—is one I have worked before in analyses of Aristotle's aesthetic and here, again, value as a perspective within which the aesthetic enjoys rules and achievements specific to it.

We are conscious of Coleridge's aesthetic idealism, his conviction that the poetic imagination can transform the given world, offering it a new and finer reality. This transformatory power of art is still the tenet at which Coleridge withholds himself from this essay's other thought-friends. In Ryle, Black, Wheelwright, and Wittgenstein we read analyses of language-work that demystify to degrees unknown in Coleridge. Yet as we follow out the implications of these analyses . . . which seek to break down rather than build up . . . we find old fascinations and assertions, suggestions, and gradually a construction.

Meinong's thought influenced Russell—who was Wittgenstein's teacher—and Wittgenstein on the question of "negative fact." Mcinong, too, asserted the reality of the false statement.

His position is true both to logic—the analysis of the intelligibility of propositions—and to psychology. When he considers contradiction in propositions, he asserts the simultaneous reality of contradictory elements in the same object. He considers the seemingly false proposition a composite of meaningful subpropositions and is thus led to believe that a whole false proposition is true by virtue of being real. This kind of conclusion reflects the inroad of psychology into the logical account, though Meinong's conclusions are not based on psychologism, the dissolution of cognitive questions into psychological ones. He maintains that the logical and psychological mutually confirm each other in the analysis of propositions. As Russell puts it, "Meinong maintains that there is such an object as the round square only it does not exist, and it does not even subsist, but nevertheless there is such an object, and when you say 'the round square is a fiction,' he takes it there is an object 'the round square' and there is a predicate 'fiction.' "[17] "I think," Russell says, that "Meinong is rather deficient in . . . instinct for reality": "To suppose that in the actual world of nature there is a whole set of false propositions going about is to my mind monstrous."

On the case of the "round square," Wittgenstein would have been with Russell. We face here what is to Wittgenstein not part of the possibility inherent in reality. In the analysis of statements of beliefs, too, Russell's position resembles Wittgenstein's and helps us to understand it. In fact, Russell attributes to Wittgenstein that discovery of the special nature of such statements, which for both thinkers is a key to the mysteries of false statement. Take the proposition, "Othello believes Desdemona loves Cassio." In fact Desdemona does not love Cassio, although the structure of such a sentence misleadingly suggests that Desdemona does love Cassio. (There is no way to construct such a double-verb belief statement in English without introducing some supposition about the reference of the subordinate verb.) We have to recognize, Russell says, that statements of belief represent belief in a proposition, not in facts and that in any case we do not believe in facts. There is no reason to see Russell in conflict with Wittgenstein here, *except* on the issue of reality. For Wittgenstein's distinction between reference to reality and reference to true or false states of affairs provides a home for "Desdemona loves Cassio" under the shelter of possibility. As we pursue Russell's notion of "negative facts," we will see that his difference from Wittgenstein on this point is important. Wittgenstein will turn out to stand between Meinong and Russell in the generosity with which he attributes existence to such facts. The *distinguos* exchanged among these three thinkers ring the subtlest and most instructive changes on a theory directly bearing on aesthetic transformation.[18]

Consider the parallel between the relation of negative fact to the external world and the relation of artwork to the external world.

This scheme shows how art and the force that creates it, imagination, can construct a special world that is not true in any usual sense, that is false in some usual sense, but that is real in some usual senses at the same time that it is false.

$$\frac{\text{negative fact}}{\text{external world}} \qquad \frac{\text{artwork}}{\text{external world}}$$

When we speak of a parallel between the two relationships, we mean that they provide models for one another, perform related gestures. Is this parallel substantial? Does our excursus into Wittgenstein, Russell, and Meinong keep us in touch with the Coleridgean base, which also posits a special reality for imaginative works? Is the negative fact—which so fascinated these three twentieth-century logicians—truly akin to the artwork? The parallels are enlightening: each model gives the other new clarity. If we think back to Ryle on imagination, we meet a source of that new clarity. By his fastidious attention to the imaging that we give ourselves in language, he characterizes the asymmetry between imager and what is imaged, between Helvellyn and the mind that images or pictures it. That asymmetry suggests a relation between picturing and pictures that in turn suggests what goes on in art and negative facts. Ryle is discussing a relation like this:

$$\text{imaging of Helvellyn} \ \rightarrow \ \begin{array}{c} \text{sense of self present} \\ \text{to Helvellyn} \\ \downarrow \\ \text{Helvellyn} \end{array}$$

And it may be that we should develop our simple and similar design into

$$\begin{array}{cc} \text{negative fact} \rightarrow \begin{array}{c} \text{positive fact} \\ \downarrow \\ \text{external world} \end{array} & \qquad \text{artwork} \rightarrow \begin{array}{c} \text{its positive} \\ \text{content} \\ \downarrow \\ \text{external world} \end{array} \end{array}$$

To begin thinking of the artwork as a negative proposition, as the statement of a state of affairs which, though real, is nonexistent, is to begin seeing how obliquely the artwork stands toward what it proposes, at what an elbow-angle it stands to that proposition. Don't we need a notion like *imagination* to explain the making of artworks, to designate a faculty establishing its worldliness through a positive proposition to which the artwork serves as a formal negation sign? *Imagination* is a useful term for this purpose. To characterize art's oblique relation to the world, we need a notion— why not call it *imagination?*—that works through an operation like metaphor, whose peculiar capacity is for transforming the world by reordering it.

Rudolf Carnap's *Pseudoproblems in Philosophy* (1928) was recently reprinted, with *The Logical Structure of the World,*[19] in a volume of surprising freshness and bearing on our theme. The term *pseudoproblems* suggests that the book will be devoted, like *The Concept of Mind* or Wittgenstein's *Tractatus,* to the dangers of false terms and false verbal problems. But Carnap's stress is more "anti-metaphysical" than Wittgenstein's and rests on an unrelenting empiricism. He remarks that "my more radical orientation was due, in part, to Wittgenstein's conception that metaphysical sentences are meaningless since they are in principle unverifiable."[20] But Carnap included much more under "metaphysical sentences" than Wittgenstein had; for instance, the "theses of reality," positions involving belief that the heteropsychological either does or does not exist independent of self, a belief that is unverifiable.

The *Pseudoproblems* assume a strictly applied empiricism, tightly (though subtly) bound to the criterion of verifiability. At first the application appears to leave less room than the *Tractatus,* not only for the aesthetic questions central here but for imaginative play in the wider sense. Yet for all that, the give in Carnap's position is especially meaningful, the more so for the texture-tightness of the fabric that is giving.

When I touch a key in my pocket, the tactile experience may suffice for knowing what the object is. My inner image of the key is dispensable in my consciousness of that object; for while that image may have psychological consequences, it adds nothing to the act of knowing. We "experience," Carnap says, "more than is necessary in order to gain the knowledge that can be obtained. . . . We can leave certain constituents of experience unevaluated . . . and our knowledge would not be diminished."[21] Our knowing establishes its laws as it goes ahead, rearranges the data in any way necessary to achieve its end, but must often ignore certain data.

All this of course is *echt*, whole-cloth empiricism. But an aperture appears in the cloth. Carnap is searching for the domain of true, "scientifically" verifiable cognitions. What kind of pseudocognitive propositions would be manufactured by recognizing that the overdetermined constituents of experience are of equal interest with the strictly cognitive elements? Carnap says that the visual image of the key remains simply "unevaluated" but is not dismissed from our experience. Art, I want to add, also accounts for the dispensable along with the essential. The painter and poet affirm what is theoretically unevaluated about the key, its visual element unneeded for cognition. This type of affirmation characterizes aesthetic propositions. Once again, as with negative facts, we find a contemporary anti-aestheticism playing toward the traditional imaginative domain.

There is an explicit distinction in Carnap between truthfulness and meaningfulness, the distinction we wrung from Wittgenstein via the negative fact: "The meaning of a statement lies in the fact that it expresses a (conceivable, not necessarily existing) state of affairs. . . . If the statement expresses a state of affairs then it is in any event meaningful; it is true if this state of affairs exists, false if it does not exist. One can know that a statement is meaningful even before one knows whether it is true or false."[22] We return directly to the *Tractatus,* and this time with a more open invitation than any Wittgenstein gave us, to seize on a model for the work of art. Meaning is the realm of slack, of possibility. In claiming this, Carnap makes a home for imaginative statements, for "objective representations," which includes far more than works of the imagination. We can at least summon to mind an empiricism so bleak that it excluded from meaning all statements that were not true. In that kind of empiricism falsehood and meaningfulness could never join company. We would know what it means for the threshold to be uncrossable between two domains of thought—

for that radical discontinuity, about which our age raps, to actualize itself.

We are brought by the present issue to Carnap's notion of object representations. With this discussion he returns to his distinction between true and false meaningful statements: "If I have a representation of a certain person in a certain environment, and if I believe that this person is now in this environment, then the representation is factual; it is either true or false. On the other hand if I merely think of that person in that environment but hold no belief concerning place or time, then I have an *object representation* . . . a factual representation can form the content of a statement, while an object representation cannot."[23] Object representations like *my son, the bird, house,* are of course used in factual statements; but they can—dependent on the intention with which we read them—simultaneously be taken as hypothetical, as fictive. Within the expression, "My son looks so and so," there is the possibility of our attending simply to *my son,* to that noun as object. Carnap refers to another example of his point, this time referring to a digression by which we fill out the words of a factual statement. Our mental representation, he says, may depict a bench as being green when we hear the sentence, "That bench is small." In this case our object representation may be unprompted by anything in the original statement. It may be adding to that statement in the way the retention of dispensable elements in cognition added to, but without changing, the theoretical cognition of a key.

Carnap's point is this: that the aesthetic, the nonrepresentational, is what is left over after the theoretically cognitive has been affirmed; and at that price he is willing to provide special housing for the aesthetic. We can see into one genesis of this concession and further into our open-text arguing if we turn here to our last display-mind, Gottlob Frege—to his "On Sense and Reference" (1892) and "The Thought: A Logical Inquiry" (1918–1919). In both of these essays he works with something like Carnap's objective representations, writing in the earlier piece that "the reference of a proper name is the object itself which we designate by its means; the idea, which we have in that case, is wholly subjective. In between lies the sense (*Sinn*), which is indeed no longer subjective like the idea, but is yet not the object itself."[24] In the later essay he works with the same triad: idea (or thought), reference, and sense. There he attributes ideas to individuals, but places "thoughts" beyond ideas in an impersonal realm. Sense, however, he continues to locate "in between." *Sense* is the term for us to follow.

In discussing logic and translation Frege finds "three levels of difference between words, expressions, or whole sentences": "The differences may concern at most the ideas, or the sense but not the reference, or, finally, the reference as well."[25] It is the ideal of translation to carry across as much as possible of these three levels. In his essay "The Thought," however, he has anticipated a problem that bears on the intelligibility we understand art to have: "The constituents of language . . . make the translation of poetry very difficult, even make a complete translation of poetry almost always impossible, for it is in precisely that in which poetic value largely consists that languages differ most."[26] That in which such value consists is heavily *sense,* the intermediate element. Though in his earlier essay Frege had been optimistic about the possibility of translating all but ideas, now he finds sense the hardest part of the poem to translate.

Translation is our best test of the essential in literary art because it isolates what cannot be disassociated from the original work. To conclude from the text as Frege does above is to conclude that the logical and the poetic diverge sharply: "To a mind concerned with what is beautiful in language, what is indifferent to the logician can appear as just what is important."[27] The logician— as defined in this essay—is the person concerned with the conditions making truthful statements possible. (Truth is defined by referential correspondence, as far as such is possible between an idea and an object of thought.) To such a logician it is indifferent whether one says *horse* or *steed* or *cart-horse* or *mare:* "what is called mood, fragrance, illumination in a poem, what is portrayed by cadence and rhythm, does not belong to the thought." To the poet, and so to the person trying to translate him, this mood or fragrance is the poem's center.

We are both far and not far from Carnap's objective representations. Carnap had asserted that "metaphysical statements—like lyrical verses—have only an expressive function, but no representative function." In this they are like *laughing* and *music,* make no statement, thus make no claim to truthfulness. This perspective is also Frege's. He is not pushing art toward cognition. He is excluding the aesthetic from cognition. Yet it is not far from the notion of artistic language as nonsense to that of such language as a new kind of sense. When art becomes a new kind of sense we are within hailing distance of the traditional worlds of imagination and metaphor. We once again circle back toward the Coleridgean. We are, as with the negative fact and object representation, close to the mystery by which the driest *Weltanschauung* is pregnant with some mystery of self-transformation.

Frege also interests himself in the matter of intention as it enters the formation of statements. He writes of what "happens when we do not speak seriously. As stage thunder is only apparent thunder and a stage fight only an apparent fight, so stage assertion is only apparent assertion. It is only acting, only fancy. In his part the actor asserts nothing, nor does he lie, even if he says something of whose falsehood he is convinced." This reminds us of Ryle; imaging took place in the mood of simulation that Frege recognizes (it also reminds us of Diderot's *Paradoxe sur le comédien,* that text born of science finding the imaginative power inside itself): "In poetry we have the case of thoughts being expressed without being actually put forward as true in spite of the form of the indicative sentence, although it may be suggested to the hearer to make an assenting judgment himself. Therefore it must still always be asked, about what is presented in the form of an indicative sentence, whether it really contains an assertion. And this question must be answered in the negative if the requisite seriousness is lacking."[28] "Requisite seriousness" is an imprecise criterion to invoke and one Carnap would not have recognized. But Frege's concession is hard to avoid once it is admitted that poetry is partly made up of indicative statement. By refusing to take an interest in that possibility, Carnap spares himself difficulty. But Frege's willingness to discuss sense and to make more of it than Carnap did shows his wider range of susceptibilities, to the kind of real-unreal indicative world the poem establishes.

Frege's insights—like Coleridge's—go to the center of the poem and, while eschewing the lingo of transformation, nevertheless show how deeply the twentieth-century logician can pitch his understanding on the Field of Faery.

At another point in *Pseudoproblems,* Carnap introduces a sequence of nonreferential pieces or fragments—in part variations on object representations—with an eye to seeing how they become "progressively more pointless," progressively farther from the verifiable. The assumptions of his experiment interest my argument. His sequence is this: "1. 'Jupiter sits in this cloud (but the appearance of the cloud does not indicate his presence, nor is there any other perceptual method through which his presence can be recognized)'; 2. 'This rock is sad'; 3. 'This triangle is virtuous'; 4. 'Berlin horse blue'; 5. 'And or of which'; 6. 'bu ba bi'; 7. '–) (*–*'."[29] The continuum is introduced revealingly: "If the first expression of this sequence is to be considered meaningful (even if false), then it would be difficult to introduce, without being arbitrary, a criterion which allows us to divide the sequence into meaningful and meaningless expressions."[30] Once the first sentence is allowed in—as nonreferential but meaningful—there is no stopping the sequence. That letting-in is Carnap's bow toward the impossible-but-real category, which he, like Frege, allows with all its implications for an aesthetic. Carnap makes space for the self-referentially aesthetic, for that which has its form in itself.

I have noted object representation and degree of pointlessness in Carnap and the discussion of sense in Frege. The two agree on some traits of language by which it can produce meaningful false statements. Neither author claims a great deal for this potency; for Carnap, in fact, it is the empty immunity of the statement that makes no claims except on our emotions. Yet the essential is that once again an area is being cleared in which aesthetic presentation can be housed and freed.

We have been considering a group of primarily British and German philosophers: Frege, Wittgenstein, Carnap, Russell, Ryle. Russell was decisively influenced by (and influential on) the atmosphere of Cambridge, at which he was a professor. Wittgenstein too was a Cambridge don. Carnap had a central position in the Vienna Circle and in the philosophical life of the University of Vienna. Wittgenstein both learned from, and deeply stimulated, the thought of that group. Ryle was an Oxford don who drew from both the Cambridge and the Vienna traditions.

What strands bind these two centers of learning to Coleridge's thought or to the related thought of Coleridge's contemporaries?

In an essay, "The Local Historical Background of Contemporary Cambridge Philosophy," C. D. Broad points out the narrowness of Cambridge philosophy in this century: it "tends to be a thin stream confined to a rather narrow and isolated, if sometimes deep, channel, and always in danger of almost drying up for considerable periods." He points out that "philosophy in Cambridge has been almost completely out of touch with general history, with political theory and sociology, and with jurisprudence,"[31] and concludes that this unusual hothouse plant has borne excellent fruit in our century thanks to the genius of "Professor Moore, Lord Russell and Wittgenstein," thinkers who "approach the subject (of philosophy) from the side of mathematics or the social sciences or the arts."

These philosophers were brought to intellectual maturity in an environment of British Hegelians: Stirling, Ferrier, Grote, Caird, T. H. Green, Bradley, McTaggart—of whom a few, certainly the last three named, were the most respected voices in British philosophy. The Cantabrigians were on the whole opposed to the Hegelian tradition, which goes back to Coleridge and to an important sector of his intellectual world. This "going back" is part of a longer story. The Hegelianism in question had planted itself in England with Stirling's *Secret of Hegel* (1865), in which transcendence of Kant had seemed to provide a welcome perfection of the idealist position. (Caird's works present "the philosophy of Hegel as the only possible eventuation of that of Kant.") Stirling was followed by idealist philosophers who relied heavily on Hegel, to draw from him the liberation required by their own thought. But even before Stirling's work, the post-Kantians were known in England. This is most obvious in Coleridge, who drew on Fichte and Schelling. For the Cambridge professor to turn against the neo-Hegelian was also to turn against the post-Kantians, like Fichte and Schelling, who themselves "made Hegel possible."

In the broadest sense Coleridge shares his idealism with Kant, Hegel, Fichte, Schelling; in a sense broad enough, that is, to define itself off from the perspectives of empiricism, positivism, or language analysis. Kant (whom Coleridge consumed and translated) and the post-Kantians stress the generative power and ontological centrality of the human self; the limits of reason and the power in "higher forms" either of conceptualizing or of intuiting; the autonomous worth of both the aesthetic and ethical dimensions of experience. Taking these tenets as directive for British idealism, Muirhead comments, "I don't think that there is any point in the idealism of the seventies—a period when Caird, Bradley, and Green were most initiatingly active—which has not been anticipated, or even better expressed by Coleridge earlier."[32]

The Cambridge analysts turn against a tradition that includes Coleridge and the British neo-Hegelians. What position were the Vienna Circle theorists adopting toward their own philosophical past, as it coincides with the tradition against which Russell and Ryle rebelled? The case of Moritz Schlick illustrates the complexity of the problem. He claims that the Vienna School reflects the perennial concerns of philosophy, stressing that discipline is an activity rather than a theory. For Schlick—as a representative of the School—philosophy does not make statements but helps us to clarify our understandings; and in that differs sharply from natural science. In the *Tractatus* Wittgenstein draws ultimate conclusions from this position. He says that since his propositions have no meaning—but are examples of method—they themselves can be dismissed as nonsense. Schlick argues that such a limitation of philosophy to method does not cut it off from a concern with "truth," since logic and experience ultimately support one another. In fact the logician must at the same time be an empiricist if he wants to understand his own activity. In this sense Schlick wants

to keep logical positivism in the mainstream of propositional philosophy, to assert the value of its statements. But only in this sense.
His fellow positivists like Carnap tended toward a different view
of their relations to the tradition; a view of themselves as substi-
tuting—for the pseudostatements that composed that tradition—
a far more correct and modest account of reality. But by either
Carnap's or Schlick's account of the earlier tradition, there seems
little in the past to deepen our description of reality.

   Cambridge and Vienna Circle philosophy adopted critical or
hostile relations toward their own intellectual pasts. The Cambridge position reacted against a specific tradition—neo-Hegeli-
anism—and through that against a nineteenth-century tradition of
idealism that intertwined with the thought of Coleridge. In this
there was some pitting of a new tradition against the old. But that
pitting was distinctively modern, as Schlick, in his time, put it.
What is at stake when Wittgenstein pulls out the rug from under
his own propositional statements? What is at stake when philosophy views itself as concerned with the method of philosophizing
rather than with the content of its propositions? Those questions
dogged the modernity of the new Cambridge thinkers.
   If the propositional content of Wittgenstein's thought exists
in brackets, outside tradition, mustn't we say the same for any
arguments that examine the way we argue? Can such arguments
relate to a tradition of propositions—such as Coleridge's? Possibly,
but with difficulty. In the first chapter of *Principia ethica,* G. H.
Moore claims no more than methodological clarity against idealism. He hopes that the nature of reality may be ideal but denies
the validity of the arguments used to defend that ideality. In the
same way Ryle—in *The Concept of Mind*—devotes himself to the
examination of strategies rather than of propositions. Linguistic
analysis—either in contemporary British philosophy or in Vienna
Circle thought—is obviously nonhistorical and nonconceptual;
and if we are to put such thought to use for historical synthesis,
for temporal threshold crossing, we have to satisfy ourselves about
the method-problem raised here. We have to consider whether
Coleridge's type of thought *can* be grasped together with Wittgen-

stein's. (In practice this essay has *been* such a grasping. But was the essay legitimate and possible?)

In the *Investigations* Wittgenstein considers "abnormal cases" of language and the clash between image and use—all in connection with the problems of defining language games and language norms. About these abnormal cases he establishes verifiable propositions. Yet at the same time, he is illustrating the nature of the language game about which he is thinking. Is this propositional thought? Yes, in the limited sense that it can be used for what in it is conceptual. In *The Concept of Mind* Ryle maintains a similar double perspective. In his chapter on imagination he helps us to perceive what we mean by imagination, helps us to understand how we talk about it. The degree of self-consciousness in this argument is very high, and in that respect the argument resembles an aesthetic—rather than a conceptual—presentation. But Ryle is avoiding the undercutting of statement by method. Here again we have argument limitedly useable for our purposes.

To treat any kind of philosophy as simply or even mainly propositional is too easy, and is too common a trap. (The person of letters often attributes more solidity to the philosopher's thought, and less to his own, than is in either case appropriate.) To treat in this way the philosophy of a mind like Coleridge is especially trapping. In thinking, he is a poet. We see this clearly enough in his definitions of imagination. Was Coleridge also concerned with his own method in formulating the notions of primary and secondary imagination? Certainly not in the way some twentieth-century philosophers are concerned, for whom that involvement is an element in statement itself. But Coleridge frames his definitions with unusual self-consciousness. The ear of the poet is joining sounds ("dissolves, diffuses, dissipates") making images (of "echoes" and "repetitions") and employing all the rhetoric of classical philosophy—from subdistinctions to uppercase letters; and is in these ways filtering the language of philosophical propositions through unusually much of what Carnap would call emotive language. Is all this an instance of concern for method counteracting statement, or even interrelating with it?

Yes and no. Method as such is not on Coleridge's mind *as* he thinks about imagination. But the constant self-modeling through language and the constant remodeling of language through self have something in common with methodic self-consciousness. Certainly, what they have in common helps ease our concern about the return from Cambridge and Vienna to Coleridge. It suggests that the practice of this essay has been both legitimate and possible, that Coleridge as well as Ryle presents himself as thought and self-reflection interrelating.

What do we find when we make that return to the Lake Country, bearing our twentieth-century propositions and self-awareness with us? We reacquire the coherence of an aesthetic tradition, bespeaking itself—that *is* this essay—from various corners.

At the same time, we find ourselves newly aware of two points at which Coleridge's implications either feel distant or draw us back to him in understandings of ourselves. Those points are his confident placing of the work of imagination in the whole context of human consciousness—the lodging of secondary within primary imagination and of primary imagination within the Creator's Mind; and his emphasis on conscious will in secondary imagination, a seemingly difficult compacting of aesthetic and ethical categories.

First point. The secondary imagination echoes the fundamental act by which the self asserts its identity and at the same time asserts the identity of the world. It is crucial in the *Biographia Literaria* that the imagination, which makes a unified and idealized artifact in the arts, exists congruous to the act that asserts and carries out existence. We admire the scope and setting of Coleridge's assertion, its contrast with some timid visions scrutinized in this essay. "Imaging"—in Ryle's sense—is as close as the quantifiers brought us to discussing "imagination" itself, and "imaging" contained no elements that united it to anything higher than itself. There is even less interest in transcendent imagination among the other Viennese and Cantabrigians—for whom that kind of faculty presented itself either as nonsense making (in Carnap) or as unprivileged and better reduced to lesser skills (the impression Russell leaves us). On the issue of imagination the philosophers considered here will disclaim Coleridge's belief in a higher context into which the work of imagination fits. But on the other hand, they will turn with fascination—often in new terms—to elements of the work traditionally attributed to the imagination. Throughout this essay—counter to expectation—we have met a reworking of imagination's operations, in discussions of the mind's work with negative facts and real impossibilities (Frege, Russell), imaging (Ryle), objective representations (Frege, Carnap), or margin-slack (Carnap) left over from the functionally empirical. These reworkings go some distance, by indirection, toward everything in Coleridge except his insistence on the poet's transubstantiation of reality. Wheelwright—the least committedly empirical of our modern group—and even Black (with his interactive metaphor) take steps toward an aesthetic of transformation.

Second point. Volition plays a role in the accounts I have drawn from thinkers of our century. Ryle's discussion of imaging is a good example. The adopting of an oblique relation to perceived reality is a conscious act: a remembering at a distance, a putting before one, a holding up for consideration. This conscious faculty is presupposed in Carnap's study of nonsense levels, in Wittgenstein's remarks on abnormal cases, or in Black's implications that metaphor is a construct.

The quantifiers of imagination help us to understand Coleridge's secondary imagination as a whole. In particular they show us what this activity makes: a new artifact that is meaningful without being true or false and that—as G. E. Moore suggested—derives its worth from absolute value rather than from referential accuracy. A critic of language like Wittgenstein helps us understand how near form making, through strategy, is to the center of art making. In Max Black's essay on metaphor—as I have said—we see to what a great extent the analyst position is congruent with a Romantic view of dissolving and recreative language.

The mind that can dissolve and then reunify, even idealize, the elements of its experience is far from the mind that juxtaposes those elements in infinitely various, but quantitatively analyzable, combinations. How can we mediate between the two conceptions? Consider an already familiar example:

The apparition of these faces in the crowd;
Petals on a wet black bough.

What has the mind done here?

"Elements of experience" have been brought together. Has something new been made from them? The example is so simple that we see right through to the anatomy of poetry, the minimal but fully aesthetic. Something new has been made, the collocation of two separate visions. That newness has been made from the simple addition of two visions jammed against one another. Is there any mystery in this buildup into a fresh vision? The imaginable form of the given world has been reestablished, reposed. If this is mysterious, then something mysterious happens here. We are not able to analyze what has happened if analyze means to give an exhaustive account—like a mathematical formula (though the cognitive claims of even such explication need exploring). On the other hand we understand—know what makes up—the new whole. In that sense we can analyze it. It is almost as though the mystery were that there is no mystery. The plain fact is that the operations of imagining, or imaging, are not a making of something new but a showing of unexpected possibilities in what is already familiar.

We balk at a Romantic view of the mysterious operations of mind in imagination but equally resist careless demystification of the kind we find in Carnap's *Rejection of Metaphysics*. The argument of this essay has returned constantly to the possibility of an account of the art-making mind, which would respect both twentieth-century quanta and insight drawn from Romantic thought. Coleridge has had to stand for a great deal; his notion of secondary imagination has had to represent a conviction of that mysterious depth in art that was incorporated in Wordsworth's "strange seas of thought," Shelley's Greek choruses, and Kleist's love-drunk waves. In this larger sense, what Coleridge has stood for still stands, after submission to conflict and analysis. But it stands clarified, opened out, desanctified. By so standing, it helps us to climb out over what is pettily quantifying in our thought. Coleridge provides us with a resistance—against which to struggle toward aesthetic accounts that are freshly true to our contemporary situation.

The Essay As Threshold

The form of the essay has still not come into its own . . . still remains trapped in a primitive, undifferentiated unity with hard knowledge, ethics, and art.

György Lukács

This book has luxuriated in thresholds, points at which major intelligibility-zones intersect, throwing up at us that seam of difference in which we find room for knowledge. (The intersections have been such as appear between the continuous and the discontinuous universe or—within those universes—between imagination and logic, originals and translations.) To know is to see difference, not to dissolve the intelligible in your knowledge but to sharpen its profile in that knowledge. Each essay has given itself to a particular threshold uncovering and threshold crossing, to an assertion of the continuity-over-borders that our existence stands ready to disclose to us. The discovery of these disclosures I see as a kind of testifying, daily acts of whole-world affirmation by which we assure ourselves—often below or against our conceptual denial—of the coherence of the world that lives us.

The present essay goes forward and backward at once. It confronts the large character of thresholds and testimony—the matter of this book—and in that returns and surveys. But it goes forward, first into a literary genus—the essay—and then into the anthropologies of probing, testifying, and standing where the new is coming into being.

127

The essay is both a dependent genus and one which looks in every direction toward frontiers (short story, moral tale, expository analysis) that enclose and define it.

The essay's dependence is complex. It is not that of positive literary history, the chemist's report, or a sociologist's tract. The essay does not draw most of its substance from a field of knowledge or a field of observation. For that the essay is both too lyrical and too personal, as well as insistent on controlling its material. (Lukács, in "On the Nature and Form of the Essay,"[1] insists that a great worker in the genre, trapped by dependence in his passion for major statement, sings in unique chains. Lukács is thinking of Plato, the medieval Christian mystics, and Kierkegaard.) But the essay does not exist independently of its *Stoff*—jealousy, roast pig, kustomized kars, *Kulturgeschichte*—in the way the poem or novel do. It is in its own way dependent.

The essay—in Montaigne, Bacon, Pater—is empirically grounded; while the novel—*Tom Jones, Moby Dick*—grounds the empirical, lays it out in chosen shapes, and remains true to it by controlling it. Richard Selzer writes[2]—in *bona fide*, harrowing essays—of the techniques, materials, and limitations of surgeons. In *The Magic Mountain*, Thomas Mann dealt with medical issues—pertaining to tuberculosis. But there is a difference between the medical discussions carried out in these kinds of writing. Selzer has neither freedom (nor need) to play with, to recast, his accounts of medical procedures. Of course, the microspecific tone of his imagination slants and shapes the way any given passes through him; of course, the given—*the* scalpel, *the* gown, *the* nervous smile—is never raw given, is always already, for essayist as well as *ficcionista*, other-biased-toward-self. But these are just the basic ground rules, above which we look into the specific limitations on the essayist's freedom. Selzer must respect the given as he knows it if he wants to write an essay, that genus made possible by its narrator's lodging in the empirical world. We could not read Selzer if we felt he was being untrue to what we know of surgical practice. Mann, on the other hand, has far more freedom in his dealing with *materia scientifica*. His literary argument is not dependent on the state of the medical art of his day. Nor will his argument, unlike Selzer's, grow outdated by developments in medical science; Mann can put "incorrect" or "outdated" scientific concepts into the mouths of his characters, and sidestep any other than artistic responsibility for them. Art alone will furnish the criteria for judging Mann's work. Or think of this historically. Milton's Ptolemaic astronomy is not one of our problems in valuing *Paradise Lost*—for we don't judge him on the basis of the scientific accuracy of his material, but only on the aesthetic maturity with which he constructs that material.

The essay demands artistic freedom for itself while working out its *Stoff*-dependency. Selzer will give life to *materia medica* by the textual energy of his work. Montaigne, Bacon, and Tom Wolfe will do the same. That ruminative flow which defines their genus will in each of these essayists be harnessed to rhetoric, strategies, aesthetic ellipses, finally to larger imaginative shape; and will in that way further substantiate Lukács' point—that while confessing itself as dependent, the essay at the same time insists on its aesthetic rights. The peculiarity of the genus lies in this vital dependency.

So the essay is of blended character. More could be said to this point, especially about the mixture of the conceptual with the sense-impressional in the genus. (Theodor Adorno tries to exhaust that matter in his inexhaustible essay, "Der Essay als Form."[3]) This mixture swirls around the essay's center—its axis of gravity— at just the point where the imaginative-empirical polarity revolves. The empirically, the repertorially dependent is in the essay grafted to its sensuous and anticonceptual element. At the opposite poles dance imagination and the conceptual, twinned (if here separate) mastery-functions, shaper-principles. (These two mastery poles arc the logical rigor and imagination twinned in the discussions of our fifth essay, on imagination and quantity—a new confirmation of the closeness of imagination to thought-rigor, and vice versa.)

In its blended condition the essay exists as testifying, its inclination that of discovering its own name in the openness where fate has left it. Montaigne, Bacon, Lamb, Pater, Wolfe: all claim attention here for their careful occupation of a ground that is uncomfortingly transitional, though in a wider sense it is that mind-zone in which the whole human condition finds itself—rudderless sailing in the amniotic sac of being, learning the direction from

the directions already taken. Theodor Adorno stresses this ontological setting in his essay on the essay, where he finds the absence
of conceptual lodging a trademark of the genre, of its author's
constant repositing of new conceptual bases for himself. Voice
management in the essay teller may be our clearest guide to the
nervy enterprise of this new genus, which, like the novel, had its
birth in the birth of middle-class curiosity, but which, unlike the
novel, was refused the baptisms of pure form, the Fielding or
Flaubert who would simply make art of the passing.

Montaigne is a launching point, for he launches himself. "Des
Cannibales" opens, in Florio's words,

> At what time King Pyrrhus came into Italy, after he had surveyed the
> marshalling of the army which the Romans sent against him: "I wot not,"
> said he, "what barbarous men these are (for so were the Grecians wont to
> call all strange nations), but the disposition of this army which I see is
> nothing barbarous." So said the Grecians of that which Flaminius sent into
> their country, and Philip, viewing from a tower the order and distribution
> of the Roman camp in his kingdom under Publius Sulpitius Galba. Lo how
> a man ought to take heed lest he overweeningly follow vulgar opinions,
> which should be measured by the rule of reason and not by the common
> report.
>   I have had long time dwelling with me a man, who for the space of
> ten or twelve years had dwelt in that other world, which in our age was
> lately discovered in those parts where Villegaignon first landed, and sur-
> named Antartike France.[4]

I include the opening and then one sentence from the second
paragraph, for in the pleat preceding that paragraph—and which
only it makes visible, as sitting does a lap—we hear the nonfictional
of this narrator, as well as his refusal of a merely expository strategy.
The first paragraph consists of two example-filled sentences—dealing with the appearance-truth split—and one moral precept. This
succession alerts us to the voice's empirical anchoring, and its vision
of truth. But to this point, up to the end of the first paragraph, we
could be dealing with a literary character whose voice the author
would then frame in some higher-order perspective. (Either the

author or a character could reflect on and ironize the words of the first paragraph's narrator.) However the fourth sentence—which opens the second paragraph—cuts off the narrator from any literary character's voice. Montaigne himself puts his first paragraph to use for a direct statement, one which—"I have had long time. . . ."— leaps off the page into directness. No *ficcionista* could reduce to a character the speaker of this sentence, which breathes its refusal to be taken even as a persona-voice, to be separated by any indirection from Montaigne's own voice. It is clearly Montaigne who is launching out into his points, shoring his argument with the data of antique bellography.

Testifying? The essayist's stance—Montaigne's—is in fact daring. Historically speaking, it broke the style-formal rites of the Greco-Roman Western dispensation, making itself part of the reader's spatiotemporal present. Think of Nash, Sir Philip Sidney, or Du Bellay as relatively foregrounded sixteenth-century voices and contrast with them the canny directness of Montaigne. Montaigne (and his successors) comes out onto us relatively unmediated—in art clothed, to be sure, yet in art that displays the artist bare as person. On the threshold of more rigid and defining genres, the essayist palps before himself as naked human. We must cross our own limits to reach him.

The point I stress here—about the essayist as open navigator—will take me later in this essay to the courages and rewards of standing across. I will go beyond or out from the essay as literary genre; from rites de passage to rites of self-transcendence, hearkening back to the world angle of Tillich's *The Courage To Be,* and of Heidegger on *ek-stasis.* I will draw up into my concluding syntax many of the *lamina mentis* functional here in earlier essays.

Addison and Steele—as even the high school junior may agree—come over the page like voices with whom. . . . They are there, stand for people, and with the seasoning of our historical sense they come to imply that eighteenth century with which one can talk, which one can find inside and recognize. (What of Milton, or Wycherly, or Bossuet lies that available in us? With them—and of course before them—we have to begin to study, to dig into the past. The limits of our historical ease will be the subject of the last essay in this book.)

Montaigne himself seems an archaism beside "I was yesterday engaged in an assembly of virtuosos, where one of them produced many curious observations which he had lately made in the anatomy of an human body. Another of the company communicated to us several wonderful discoveries, which he had also made on the same subject by the help of very fine glasses. This gave birth to a great variety of uncommon remarks, and furnished discourse for the remaining part of the day."[5] The ease of the writing defeats analysis. What resources the essay discovers in us for being what we are, bourgeois talkers and observers. What "I" could fit more comfortably inside its verbal skin than this or take us more effectively with it? (Even the "I" of the lyric poet, who sometimes speaks as if from within us—in Whitman, Cummings, Rilke—speaks of its generic condition, reminds us in process that it represents a form.) The very looseness of Addison's English is space for us to fit in, rousing ourselves to a gentle excitement at mention of the "extravagant dream." Has this gentle-crafty narrator his place in the essay's "I"-tradition?

Again, as with Montaigne, the essayist makes a move daring in its directness—the more daring for its casual dress. Addison crosses the threshold of generic expectations and talks his reader forward with him. His tone covers itself—is ironic with its *virtuosos* and *wonderful discoveries*—but is unshielded as letters, open-voiced and available. Testifying to experience, rather than to experience as art, Addison is only limitedly his own dupe, only limitedly voiced by that form which he has a chance to voice himself. The limit on him is that minimal one, language-limit; the power over him of a language that chooses him as he gives it life.

Direct testimony—"testifying"—is widely available in a high-print culture. There are letters, diaries, confessions, interviews: every kind of spillover from the relatively unmediated heart. Some of this detritus catches in the mind and feeds us, though even many ambitious compilations—*Give Sorrow Words,* Wallace Stevens' *Collected Letters,* Frank Harris' *My Life and Loves*—leave us alone with ourselves, far from the *novus homo* we expect art to make us. The essay's thresholding value lies precisely in its artistic element, in that mixed degree—Lukács again—of form-insistence and free-talk, that mixed degree we hear in Montaigne and Addison.

Charles Lamb forces us into his essay's "I":

A Dissertation upon Roast Pig

Mankind, says a Chinese manuscript, which my friend M. was obliging enough to read and explain to me, for the first seventy thousand ages ate their meat raw, clawing or biting it from the living animal, just as they do in Abyssinia to this day. This period is not obscurely hinted at by their great Confucius in the second chapter of his Mundane Mutations, where he designates a kind of golden age by the term Cho-fang, literally the Cook's holiday. The manuscript goes on to say, that the art of roasting, or rather broiling (which I take to be the elder brother) was accidentally discovered in the manner following.[6]

There is the grammatical "I"—"my friend M.," "which I take to be the elder brother,"—that risks no confusion with the "I"s of "Call me Ishmael," or "Depuis longtemps je me suis couché de bonne heure." Lamb's "I" is itself the framing insight into his text, is therefore not available to that text as a character or means of argument; whereas the grand "I" of prose fictions is never too grand to be applied, never too invulnerable to give off the scent of its author's control. There is also the deep "I", the submerged "I" of Lamb's essay tone. To hear it we have to back off, as often we must back off from the words of a conversation before we truly hear what is being said to us. Artifice there is in this deeper voice, but it is that of a single other voice conversing us into it, making no effort at conveying fragments of an artifice, above all not of an extended world with its own spatiotemporal freedom.

The essayist's freedom to associate, to play out the mind, is proverbial—and well illustrated in just the essay openings tasted here. Montaigne, Addison, now Lamb; all three claim ample mind-talk space, and rapidly—by transitions into one or another new theme—insist on their rights to zigzag, to run cross field. However, the worlds they move through are tangible, at least by the mind, and refuse any sense of having been fabricated—as do those digressive labyrinths Sterne or García Márquez take us through. Here the essay's testimony is of one returned from a consequential trip, who reports on it in deserved ease.

Two more essay instances: the first because it carries the testifying theme, the second because it proves how conservative the essay genre remains, even in an age like ours when the essay's brother, the novel, is being chewed like a bone.

First Pater's essay on Leonardo. In giving voice to impressions, Pater simply testifies. Testifying, for him, takes the place of the first person pronoun. That pronoun is of course present—in various data-directives concerning Vasari's text, or stages and transitions in Leonardo's life—but the bulk of the essay, word-conjurations before select pictures or select moods of the painter, is a prolonged revery. There is no escaping this revery while reading it; and in this Pater's work verges at times on the incantatory of narrative poetry like Tennyson or Hofmannstahl. The revery is a holding up of the beheld object, displaying it to the reader or observer. The author-narrator meanwhile converts itself into a moving perception, tracing the contours of value:

> All the thoughts and experience of the world have etched and moulded there, in that which they have of power to refine and make expressive the outward form, the animalism of Greece, the lust of Rome, the mysticism of the middle age with its spiritual ambition and imaginative loves, the return of the Pagan world, the sins of the Borgias. She is older than the rocks among which she sits; like the vampire, she has been dead many times, and learned the secrets of the grave; and has been a diver in deep seas, and keeps their fallen day about her; and trafficked for strange webs with Eastern merchants; and, as Leda, was the mother of Helen of Troy, and, as Saint Anne, the mother of Mary; and all this has been to her but as the sound of lyres and flutes, and lives only in the delicacy with which it has moulded the changing lineaments, and tinged the eyelids and the hands. The fancy of a perpetual life, sweeping together ten thousand experiences, is an old one; and modern philosophy has conceived the idea of humanity as wrought upon by, and summing up in itself, all modes of thought and life.[7]

The conservative, perhaps I should say durable, feature of the essay is its testifying, its refusal to surrender the human voice, conversational and ruminative at once—as it was already in Montaigne.

Tom Wolfe pulls the tradition toward our moment, into a bold anthropology of our tribe. His language—hyped up ironically, stretched and pulled into the tensions of the society he describes—witnesses both to its world and to itself as account. Deep in the trammels of the computer-age gyre, this voice fights any temptation to become more art than its own voice:

> The first good look I had at customized cars was at an event called a "Teen Fair," held in Burbank, a suburb of Los Angeles beyond Hollywood. This was a wild place to be taking a look at art objects—eventually, I should say, you have to reach the conclusion that these customized cars *are* art objects, at least if you use the standards applied in a civilized society. But I will get to that in a moment. Anyway, about noon you drive up to a place that looks like an outdoor amusement park, and there are three serious-looking kids, like the cafeteria committee in high school, taking tickets, but the scene inside is quite mad. Inside, two things hit you. The first is a huge platform a good seven feet off the ground with a hully-gully band—everything is electrified, the bass, the guitars, the saxophones—and then behind the band, on the platform, about two hundred kids are doing frantic dances called the hully-gully, the bird, and the shampoo. As I said, it's noontime. The dances the kids are doing are very jerky. The boys and girls don't touch, not even with their hands. They just ricochet around. Then you notice that all the girls are dressed exactly alike. They have bouffant hairdos—all of them—and slacks that are, well, skin-tight does not get the idea across; it's more the conformation than how tight the slacks are. It's as if some lecherous old tailor with a gluteus-maximus fixation designed them, striation by striation.[8]

Testifying, quite literally. Wolfe offers the eye of exactitude, names that surface complexity, which in our time has found an infinite mixed glitter. This is not the testimony of Zola or the Goncourts or Flaubert—who also witnessed to the painful *hicceitas* of detail, but who did so into a fictional web with its private spatiotemporal. Wolfe holds forth the cracked pulsing skin of his very instant, in a language that instant creates from him.

Testifying here has acquired a special and essentially literary meaning, as it had in my first essay. An essay, an *assaye,* has assumed the sense of an upward probe, a salience out from those more ritual voice-uses that include the generically formalized arts. Many of this book's examples have in fact been taken from the growths of the voice—into the ethereal elevations of a Rilkean elegy, into diverse modes of water-address, into the crossing beyond that is the moment of achievement in translation, into the mutually fructifying narratives of the Romantic poet and the plain-land positivist. In the following essay I will look at some of the names we can give our history as we try out on our mind-tongues the whole voice of the past.

Voice, then, can assume new registers, can cross thresholds—of articulation and imprecation—can establish and inhabit new worlds. The salience of language into the essay is in that sense indissociable from the entire liminal adventure of human existence. Voiced language, crossing its thresholds, will spring from the same desire all cultures make evident—to channel and inspire upwelling powers.

The rite de passage is an *assaye* in the fullest sense—and a testifying. Van Gennep in his time, and more recently Victor Turner (with his discussions of liminality in primitive culture as well as ours) made us conscious of those rituals attendant on social or personal transition: from fetus to infancy; from unmarried to married; from prepubertal to pubertal; from life to death: rituals hallowing, protecting, and giving dignity to our vulnerability in radical change. Turner has gone farther, recently, into the physiognomy of the chosen liminal figure—the shaman, hippy, ascetic—who becomes for his/her culture a representative reminder of social limit and its crossability.

Thresholds and testifying have been my interworking motifs. Terms like these surge upward into expressive relief, off the ground-base of language as naming (just as language itself is an ecstatic high, a soaring-over promoted upward from things by themselves—using man as medium). Thresholds are points defined by crossings that are themselves uncertain of their destination. I have been concerned with two different aspects of such crossings: the transacted intersection itself—in which a force reaches, crosses, and situates itself on the far side of a threshold, salutes, waves its hat—testifies to being in a state of crossing. In my discussions of imagination and of the argument of water, one modality of expression or one thought was brought close to another, brought into that burning light of juxtaposition by which we could read the author's testimony to new congruence (testimony remaining here, as ever, the product of an ambiguous and luring passion—to affirm, to posit). My other discussions touched different forms of going up to the threshold and testifying. Untranslatability forced me to deal with the act of translation, which assembles various versions around an original, like drones around a queen. (The translations of a single work form a palimpsest over it, a weave of striations through which the original is partially visible.) Translation in this sense is neither fully transactional—for it remains outside the work translated—nor of that simpler up-to-here-no-further character that draws together statements within lyrical poetry and logical analysis. Translation closes toward its original, endures a certain interpenetration of substances, but stands apart as testimony. To these instances I contrast the full-bodied transaction central to my second essay—"Beauty As the Threshold of Nature with Art." There I looked at a speculative world-frame—self, nature, beauty, ascent—in which interpenetrative transactions were invited as the rule. All was to be permeable by all. Spiritual monism supposed a single world substance in which even the evil-good polarity washed away into shadings and degrees. Beauty making through art provided Plotinus—as it did Marcel, Stokes, and Rilke—with the clearest instances both of testifying and of threshold crossing. Nature—the rock, the log, the deeply seen landscape—passed through the artist's yearning imagination, upward into a new-world beauty conferred on it. Beauty making, the instant of that radiance, was the art maker's testimony to his achievement. It was a testifying to being-in-the-world, the simple exercise of which was, in this sense-domain, a producing of beauty.

I have stretched the threshold concept, but with concern for its center, the point that holds its elasticity. Thresholds are criteria for our ability to expose ourselves to the unpredictable, as well as to note the fruitful boundaries in our lives. Recognition of thresholds, either in ourselves or in others, is practice in thinking in advance, in anticipating—so as to control—whatever is just coming into fruit. Testifying is the proof we can give of our willingness to practice.

Death informs all threshold and testimonial thinking. As a (seemingly) final threshold, death in fact copies that first threshold over which we pass into earthly existence. Death waits for us inside us, with patience and a finger pointed—toward that *limen* we know because we crossed it earlier from one world into the next. Living death effectively, as what Rilke calls "life's other side," we promote in ourselves the ability to deal with our transitory and staged condition, and we prepare our voices for a loud hallelujah before the (seemingly) final threshold crossing.

Threshold awareness, then, is a sense of consonance in opposites, a growing together in mutuality of many important thought and existence-zones which inform our lives. We don't want to say—*condamnés à mort avec des sursis indéfinis* as we are—that we can take the measure of our existence, identify its core, the collapsible structuring of our human universe. In fact as thinkers, essayists, namers we take our existence-cue from what Heidegger calls *ek-stasis,* a standing out from ontological mereness. We too are upstarts, upsurges, by nature incapable of any perspective back onto an outfolded universe, onto measurable contours and extents. Consonance of opposites, wherever we see it, is precisely what lets itself be seen by our condition; which is itself a continual drawing together of comparables.

Death is the limit condition for argument and learning. Threshold par excellence, death—our collective and each individual's personal death—demands of us testimony and testifying, insists on itself as the interrogation of all prior and lesser crossings. By opening my discussions with untranslatability I meant to show a thought-bias, an educated sense that all borders—including death's—can be crossed. I approached obliquely, showing that there is no adequate—that is, internal—proof of untranslatability. By implication I suggested there can be no adequate internal proof of death as obliteration, as border-nonborder. In subsequent essays I either supported that implication or shored it up quietly, leaving it unchallenged. Discussing Plotinus and Stokes I paid allegiance to a whole *kosmos* amply opening its telos to the artist, sacrificing itself upward to spiritual self-refinement. Testimony like Van Gennep's—to the universal pretechnological belief in afterlife, and to the import of crossing well equipped—would have attached itself comfortably to either of these first two essays.

Later essays danced around death, rarely naming it. The two central essays on language—which composed the second part—stressed both diversity in language use and the convergence of diverging systems upon nameable zones (like the lyric poem) or themes (like water as preempted by our experience of it). The life of this analysis pointed ever to intelligibilities—congruences, mesh-areas—where there might have seemed to be random diversity. In this sense—but that, of course, is my base assumption — these discussions of language challenged death the dissolver. To the extent that death is entropy, death can be fought off word by word, in that praxis of "telling about it" which Foucault and Barthes insist on. That kind of praxis was the display-casing for the third essay, an interlude of fragments in which I testified to my understanding of the Plotinian aesthetic—by permitting matter's upward procession through the name itself. Testifying—about which this book turns as it discusses thresholds—was at that point an effort to admit death-as-limit into another orifice of the argument. A book of concepts even free, even associative like this one—forever threatens itself with false innocence, as though able to guarantee its author a strange "diplomatic immunity" from his or her commitments. Imaginatively fused language—passionate document-chunks—lie into the argument as pleas for the author's incorporation, as protests against the author's exclusion from his own work. At the least, then, my third essay guarantees the book's discomfort with the unitoned discourse its *Stoff* requires of it. Death—in true descent from (seemingly) ultimate death—will sing inaudibly through whatever efforts we make to talk death down through the wholeness of our song.

Death. The present essay's swelling concern with the topic grows out over its own edges into a final essay on literary-historical thresholds. That essay will speak for itself soon. We will taste the problem of limits as we grasp—both discovering and inventing—the cultural past that lies around us and behind us. What we will find, reaching out into that limit-field, is that our mere entry into it throws upward from within us the hermeneutic *oy vey* of palping, the testifying with some exactitude to just the point we reach. That testifying itself will be sufficiently death's other side that it will bring the breath rushing from death.

Testifying, as we now begin to say, equates to experiencing death as master-limit, master-threshold, and perhaps master-challenge. This essay opened as an essay on the essay and folded into itself samples from that genus in which—starting from mind naked, mind in the middle—man or woman works through probes of the shape of the world, coming out not against the limits of form but against the limits of thought and expression, their pressure against the human condition. Against that nongenus description I laid a few comments on the rite de passage in archaic cultures; on the protective *Feierlichkeit*—dignity and pomp—with which mankind accompanies various passages through the fire of time. The essay is the modern person's rite de passage, truly an *assaye*. And in being *rite,* the essay too mounts to the limits our condition allows to impose themselves on us. Those limits, the ceiling, are where our need to testify takes place.

The act of testifying speaks to that awareness of the other— of unmasked otherness, death—which typically becomes the place of self. To testify: to be a witness. What better term for the goal of our highest strivings? Making ourselves a witness, saying the words that compose an *ars bene moriendi,* noting the totality of existence from the highest ground available to us, so as truly to say and feel with Spinoza, *non ridere, non lugere, sed intelligere:* all this, if kept to the human and free from the mechanized, will constitute the highest stance—even the nearest to an *imitatio Christi*—available to our kind at this time. I often reconsider my preference for *testifying* over terms like *expression* or *imagining* as accounts in which to place the work of art. A particular example helps me. Why do I make those images of myself whose growing pulls at my life, tears my time from me? Why children? I think we procreate in order to prove our own existence to ourselves, to testify to having been here. So shallow and transitory is the transition of life, for all the thresholding that slows and signalizes it! So great is the desire to believe in our own existence! We give birth as testimony! We testify equally by voicing ourselves nakedly and continuously out into the limit death becomes in the making of the essay. Testifying to ourselves—as Montaigne or Tom Wolfe—we believe in what we are, not—as happens with Joyce or Céline—in what art makes us produce of it. The essay, assaying, is par excellence our notch in the tree of reality.

Limits in the Time
of Consciousness

> This human mind wrote history, and this must read it. If the
> whole of history is in one man, it is all to be explained from
> individual experience.
>
> Emerson, *Essays*

I have stood at a variety of thresholds: between original text and translation of it; between nature and soul
at the point where beauty announces itself; between
the arguments of logical positivists and the mechanics of lyric
poetry; among scientific, aesthetic, and religious zones of language;
and finally on the threshold between the essay and the opposite
poles of imagination and empirical dependency. The common concern in these inquiries is with that transition-instant in which the
glare of new meaning asserts itself, and in some sense a *novus homo*
stands on the far side refreshed. I am not dealing with epiphanies—
the term is too grand—nor certainly with that flash of verity, that
surprised-by-joy of C. S. Lewis. I am dealing with reminders to
our fallen day of the *mysterium tremens,* of what the rite de passage
has to have given the primal person in us—from Borneo to
Ketchikat.

In the present chapter I return to considerations from an
earlier essay—"Shamans in Turtlenecks."[1] I remarked there that in
reassuming our pasts we rapidly reach limits beyond which neither
learning nor intuition can take us. We find that we have lost the
voice-sound, the meaning of the ancient profile, the essentials of
the older perspective. At the time of writing that essay I was

wrestling with the implications of a classics career. For fifteen years I had been teaching Greek and Latin literatures with predictably disappointing results. I had assumed that the problem lay with classical studies—its dusty methods, its conservatism, its uncertainty of purpose—rather than with the classical material itself. (Several years in the Mediterranean world had left me no doubt that Winckelmann's radiant Antiquity had cut a light into History. I will never doubt that.) However, with increasing contemporary experience, and with fresh respect in my own writing for the currencies of language, I began to question the availability of the entire Greco-Roman experience. I wondered—for a while this difficulty seemed crucial—why ancient (especially Greek) humor seemed so hard to locate, let alone appreciate. (For too long I had forced myself to force students to laugh at Homer's *outis* joke. I had recommended Stanford's analyses of such humor, but without conviction. They were useless.) I wondered why Greek tragedy (the genre) seemed—in the long run—too stylized to catch me, both too tragic and too inspiring to mean my life. I wondered— and this hurt—why Archilochos (at one end) and Herondas (at the other) were the only kinds of Hellene I was able to feel on my skin. Plato particularly escaped me. And so forth. The Greco-Roman material as a whole began to seem a threshold I could not cross. The more I "learned" about it, the farther it receded.

What can we say about the knowability of ourselves as history? What we can say must be formulated against the screen of that *ourselves*. History—human culture inserting itself in each of us as memory and consciousness—is the other instructively only because it exists in and through us, its radical subjects. We form and endure our history, invent and discover it at the same time—in the puzzling dance of subject with object that forms the composite of reality. Were that history not already inside us—in some sense which invokes Jung as well as Hegel—we would be unable to recover it, though were it totally inside us, which it is not, there would be no it for us to recover.

Knowing ourselves thoroughly, we might know the totality of ourselves-as-history, become identical with the entire human experience. We might account for the peculiar this-side-that-side nature of our access to the historical. When we assert that we cannot get past Bacon, or Boccaccio, or Hammurabi—in our backward clearing of space for the intelligible—we implicitly place ourselves deeper into time than these thresholds that test (and perhaps defeat) our comprehensions. Consider any of the ways we build visual or mental perspective; by looking at the moon's surface with the "knowledge" of its globe shape, or by looking at a flat, opaque sea-surface with "knowledge" of what lies under it, deepening it. Historical events or conditions, far-horizons, as they may be, of what is intelligible for us, are like these interpretable phenomena—are not one-dimensional Potemkin Villages but are for our experience outer surfaces of a rounded totality; a totality that we would need to embrace before declaring it unembraceable.

This rounded totality—which assures us there is a backside, a fulness even to the horizon—is always present in the form of a world. Against a foreground of studious palpings—through the minima of literary or art history, through the fossil record, through the astrophysical history of the solar system—we have to suppose a backdrop of worldlike totality, a roundness. That supposition is the enabling condition of knowledge.

In translating, which we know as always approximate testimony, we address the original text as both uncrossable limit and as sharer with us, in a global context, which makes sense of both of us. (In an earlier essay I wrote of a "third language," intelligibility, which grounds the original's and my relation to one another. My present drift is similar, though now I jettison the third-language metaphor and work more closely with the globe of Being.) A Tlingit potlatch poem will not simply be intelligible to such and such a degree, as I approach it through my language, but it will be "capable of being translated" even as we discover that in the process of finding the poem "untranslatable," of finding the far side of the poem. (This was the substance of the first essay.) Translation serves here as art-model for the entire process of comprehensions, modeling the global presuppositions on which knowledge depends. Not only in translation, though, is the obduracy of the threshold softened by the wholeness-sense we bring to our crossing; the softening also occurs in that inward understanding which ritual patterns, placing us even in our origin on the far side of the last threshold to be crossed. What lure of self-transcendence—we ask Plotinus or Stokes—lies in the self-enclosed granite, as it awaits the crying vision that will release it? What but the conviction that a Phidian version of Zeus lies on the far side of it, breaking sky for the angels? Matter to be formed also contains the knowledge of what that matter can be formed into. Similar round-world assumptions pertain to my two essays on the relations between poetic and discursive-analytical language. The backside or framing of each language—whether of positivism, theology, lyric poetry, or literary criticism—is a global discourse (like Heidegger's *Sein,* which guarantees *Denken* through *das Wort*) that has to be presupposed before the nexus of diverse language relations is explained and untangled. This is not simply the presupposition I brought to looking at various account-languages, but it is in each of them pregnant in that very language's sense of being distinct, of existing against a ground. My discussion of the essay dealt with these same factors in threshold crossing. I concluded by considering the essayist's individual *assaye* a direct scraping of the roof of intelligibility. Shielded by none of the hallowed genres, the essayist was forced to invent his form, limits, and diction against the blue sky. Here he faced death, in ultimacy. Here his patience with time became testimony. What lured such testifying from Montaigne, Pater, or Wolfe except their knowledge, against knowledge, that utterance is at least its own response, that expression and *tò 'ón* which completes it, meet one another like corresponding hemispheres of a bell jar?

Not, I was born but, I got a Fulbright—to Greece.

Born, of course, was already touching the first cause. It was swimming up to the surface drowned in knowledge of what becoming human has always been. It was starting out, with the inevitable already somewhere in mind.

I was born to academic culture (of finesse, of humane-classical-Montaignian turn). The mind was open and keys to its growth—in language, discourse, music—lay waiting on the table. What then seemed essential and textured—wading through schools and disciplines to the threshold of an academic career—now seems of a moment, preparation for a journey out into overseas others that would put the historical threshold against me. Primitive enough to long, I longed for my origins.

Greece was not the first place where I encountered human culture up against either its own origins or nature as grounding limit. In an Illinois childhood I was forcing my eyes against glacial moraines near which—ten thousand years before—early Americans had camped and built. The challenge posed by this experience had led me to think of the Beresovna Beast and the Pleistocene Dawn as part of our shared cultural landscape. William Golding's *The Inheritors* read itself off like *veritus incarnata*, my own achievement.

In Greece I hit the privilegedly historical and was to think Maurice Mandelbaum's *Problem of Historical Knowledge* from the page directly onto the marble. Nothing about Greece acquired its full interest until what was primitive and prior there had begun its speech; but while I listened, the Parthenon gave at once, light streaming from rational passion. A prime Greece lay behind—and behind Greece itself lay the first walls of time. What did that first have to say to me?

Take Kuaua (near Albuquerque) for simplicity's sake, for an example of that first. It is mid-August, 107 in the shade, as you drive into the parking lot. Around you lie the ruins of a once highly developed pueblo culture of the thirteenth century. (All these terms are rinsed with compromise, betray in their tuftiness my efforts to get under and behind my language. *Ruins,* to start with. The Romantic of the word outweighs its needed vocation, to stress erosion as natural rather than as a cruel disappointment. The Kuaua ruins, strong and rusty with heat, refute any *lacrimas rerum.* "Once highly developed" must also be cut to size, as it is taken from the "Glory that was Greece" mode. Efforts like these clear ground for the Kuaua before us this day in August 1978. We must be able to *hear* a cricket, to *see* a seed.) You concentrate this culture into yourself, making of its vestiges a talk inside you; then hit the Kuaua Museum—that vestige-nucleus—where you bridge as you can into

the world people made for themselves seven hundred years before—in the adobe outside. You are there, and here, at a threshold
into the house of your past.

Standing at that threshold requires the silence of training—
as will standing on the threshold of a fresh translation from a new
original; or of a fresh transformation of "natural material" into the
beauty of art; or of a new *ek-stasis* profile evoked in you by the
essay you testify with. The silence of training will be more an
openness to the voice you let the past employ for you, and yet that
silence will not come to the first instant of attention. It will be
swamped by the noise of the blood and by restive veins. You have
to go farther in, to the outward!

On the doorway of the house of your past—this time—you
find cases of minima: seeds, nuts, dried plants; hollow gourds;
worked flints; skin pouches; colored pebbles. What little these
pueblo dwellers left was what they had from the ground around
them and worked, and what they turned into the essential games,
water carriers, fire starters, energy storers. I was able to find their
economy, their necessary thrift, in me. Working with little—stingy
but barely adequate natural products—they had been able to support themselves and build a civilization. (Bandelier, in his great
bad novel *The Delight Makers,* intuits what we can make ours from
that civilization.) I who at this moment strip myself to the minima
of my possessions, divest myself of house and car, and travel as
light and thin as I can—haven't I, in recommencing—all I need
inside to assess that fertility-in-frugality which the Kuauans built
with?

From this dogged agreement grew numerous affinities, which
I sight from the threshold formed against my horizon by Kuaua.
An astringent, god-peopled sky is sandblasted back, unremitting
heat. Dry joy sears up from daily tasks, purpose—in need—turns
every wheel. Final values hover ever implicit. Ego and community
take double toll, doubly give life—in what will have to have been
deep passages in the sun. Farther I go by stepping out into the
site; and then, shortly after, by testing the round-world hypothesis.

Into the site means envelopment by the site. (I remember the
fiasco of my first year in Greece, as wet archaeologist trying to
evidence-think my way back into sherd-holes like Gla, Asine, or

"ancient Thebes." With despair I look back on the rubble-heap agglomerations of work in *The American Journal of Archaeology*, trivial positivism too poopless to raise an ant—let alone an architrave.) Envelopment—"data" are thin on this ground—has to mean thinking that asperity of life, museum artifacts now, squarely back into daily use, in this (presumed) cooking chamber here, in that (presumed) dormitory room there, in this or that storeroom. Anasazi Indian man and woman have to peel off your skin into those enclosures that require you to complete them. In that *require* lies the critical Plotinian *epistrophe,* the turning back. Once that reappropriation has announced itself by its claim on you, the landscape, too, will permeate you with its eye. You will begin to feel yourself a vision of those cottonwood trees bluely cool down there against the shrunk Rio Grande, against a far caked horizon of shimmering maize and dust. You will be a given as well as a giver, and in position to hail onto yourself the round-world totality which Kuaua in its time, and you in your Kuaua-time, must imagine containing you both.

I want to linger on the matter heralded in "Anasazi Indian man and woman have to peel off your skin into those enclosures that *require* you to complete them." The *require* turn is eventful.

To know is to know in affinity and congruence, to touch the brotherhood of the other. Not to know, to find unintelligible, is to reach the alien, that which does not respond and even to do that only from the center of the intelligible. I—you, we—live in varying degrees of intelligibility, various gradings off into darkness. Implicit in this working assumption lies another: that knowing in intelligibility is *making* affinity, is *creating* the intelligible world—of our history, of our material constitution, of our supraterrestrial origins. In *this* tenet, I realize, slippery-slope logic pushes us toward great world-making themes like Fichte's or Schopenhauer's and tends to leave us stranded with the universes our minds have created. Kuaua—to bring it home—will rise before us subjects as a plateau of need or imagination. At this point, of course, the alarm bell will sound and the objective-worlders will surge in—insisting that consciousness transcends itself into its objects of knowledge—

finds itself guaranteed by them. What evidence have these objectivists? I rest my own argument on the experience networked through me by the above *require,* on experiences of that "being solicited" which mark all establishment of objects for knowledge and experience, and which should allay the objectivist fear. The logical limitations of raw experience, as a defense for a philosophical position, seem to me quickly overcome by a look at alternative—especially purely logical—grounds for defense.

The above *require* fans out over this book, which has depended on ontological solicitation for the event-patterns it considers. Translation was viewed as a response to a challenge, a testimony to the object-text, as much as a reestablishment of that text. The point, however, was more exact; the testimony in translation was what evoked the original's challenge, and yet it did not for that reason invalidate the challenged text's response. *Require*—to pursue the matter—was written all over the objects freed into their form by the Plotinian or Stokesian sculptor. Art was not laid onto nature but, coming first from the artist met a simultaneous *nisus* in the granite. What else than a *require* seems implicit in the draw of various "languages of water" toward a lingua franca they represent or "articulate distinctively." Another answer is imaginable, that in fact the draw is a fiction created by retrospective juxtaposing of these languages. But with such an alternative we return to an ultimate perspective-schism between views of what is necessary for different thought-modes to be brought together in reflection. What, finally, about the place of *require* in the work of the essayist? Historical constraints are everywhere on this writer . . . from the limits of his language, from the pressure of surrounding genres—but these are simple restraints rather than solicitings. From the ceiling come—once the essayist has conceded to them inwardly—voices that I take to be self freshly presented as the critical and generic ear of mankind. From that hearing—which his need finds truly there—the essayist derives his only (and sufficient) *require.* That outer for him will under the best conditions be less guiding than the outer of, say, the writer of short fictions, for whom inherent form is already present as one kind of telos.

I have confronted the historical threshold through an archaic Kuaua-instance; arguing with thin data and thick intuition.

(Geertz' thick description is kin to thick intuition, and helps fix the point here.) I have tried to ground our gift for crossing to the archaic living-cluster, though I was aware of the unprovability of my effort. Nothing I found will alleviate what is pure hope and assertion in this critical thesis, though experience—solace and instructor—will finally put the test question, Has time given us a growing or diminishing sense of intimacy with our archaic knowledge-object? Time will have to take the place of "finds."

What about the *limes* of less distant historical thresholds, the subtler issues raised by zones of our history where we in fact rediscover our own scent? Or by those—possibly even closer to us in time—from which we feel excluded? What can we say about these patterns of light and shadow, these zones of substance and danger-distance?

In the essay "Shamans in Turtlenecks," to which I referred above, I drew threshold lines between Addison and Steele and Milton, or again between Horace and Archilochos. In each instance—and I kept pressing farther backward toward the "dark of culture time"—I was testing the limits of familiarity, the increasing loss of what could be tonally taken for granted. There was—as I went farther back—a devolution of the Western poetic voice into some distant echo chamber.

I now find those threshold lines too hastily drawn, and my earlier conclusions—about what we can or cannot recapture of the culture-past—limited. I had relied too boldly on the meaning-muffling role of time, and I had neglected the role played in the past-knowing act by the simple exercise of that act. Not knowing is never pure exclusion from the object of knowledge but forever creates itself as a more or less enlightened stage of knowing. Attempting to know even the remotest culture-past, Kuaua or Les Eyzies, is by its nature attempting to penetrate limits buried deeply within us.

I want to experiment again—but with a new *limes*—and once again, as I did in "The Argument of Water," to create a small *musée imaginaire,* through which to enrich my conclusions on the penetrability of the archaic.

Method and material will determine the construction of this museum, and will propose one another. The material will be seven poetic texts drawn from earlier time-zones, reaching (in order) from our age "backward" toward texts of such antiquity and isolation that, like Kuaua itself, they must virtually furnish their own explanation. Material like this proposes, as the criterion of its availability to us, the question whether or not we can "translate" it. (Translate, in this wider sense, means "render intelligible in our own voice," or in some extension of ourselves from which we can learn. Pope's Homer is a translation, still for us today; Rieu's *Four Gospels* never was and never will be a translation.) Translation, in testing the limits of its usefulness, naturally hungers toward the ancient. And in so doing—as I argued in "Translation and Criticism" in *The Knife in the Stone*—the translator engages with critical-interpretative problems more directly than either the critic or the historian. Text translation, word engaging word, is the most unsentimental test of our readiness for stages of our past.

What stance—once again—belongs to the opening of the translation? What I said of Kuaua needs restating. One does not burst in, even against a fifties Gary Snyder poem, nor does one read it—familiar as the language may be—without at the same time translating it. A space-clearing is required in which to put the fresh text. In that sense reading, which presupposes freedom and askesis, becomes translation whenever the read text presses "foreignly" away from one's base language. However, this distinction can be misleading. I may read-translate Gide more easily, with less linguistic effort, than I give to Joyce. I may want to say that in reading I translated Joyce but not Gide.

I open the museum with a poem from Gary Snyder's *Back Country*, published in 1957.

A Walk

Sunday the only day we don't work:
Mules farting around the meadow,
                        Murphy fishing,
The tent flaps in the warm

Early sun: I've eaten breakfast and I'll
                             take a walk
To Benson Lake. Packed a lunch,
Goodbye. Hopping on creekbed boulders
Up the rock throat three miles
                             Piute Creek—
In steep gorge glacier-slick rattlesnake country
Jump, land by a pool, trout skitter,
The clear sky. Deer tracks.
Bad place by a falls, boulders big as houses,
Lunch tied to belt,
I stemmed up a crack and almost fell
But rolled out safe on a ledge
                             and ambled on.
Quail chicks freeze underfoot, color of stone
Then run cheep! away, hen quail fussing.
Craggy west end of Benson Lake—after edging
Past dark creek pools on a long white slope—
Lookt down in the ice-black lake
                             lined with cliff
From far above: deep shimmering trout.
A lone duck in a gunsightpass
                             steep side hill
Through slide-aspen and talus, to the east end,
Down to grass, wading a wide smooth stream
Into camp. At last.
             By the rusty three-year-
Ago left-behind cookstove
Of the old trail crew,
Stoppt and swam and ate my lunch.[2]

From the outset I feel on foreign ground, decide to begin
here my sequence of back-receding thresholds. (Snyder's piece is
not too close to my moment—not yet high-tech involved, not yet
part of late-century economics, not quite nuclear-aware, not yet
feminist—yet, for I am fifty-six at this writing, his language tones
in to fifties awarenesses that even the sky-walkers among us must
still feel under the skin. We are post-McCarthy in this poem, not
yet at *The Greening of America*. We are with that wagon train of
the beat digression, which stopped in the Mountains.)

Let's read a little, translating. Snyder's easy language, we see,
is at once made hard by telegraphic syncopations; variations in
enjambment, hard arresting proposals—"a lone duck in a gunsight-

pass"—and finally—to jump to the end then back into the beginning—by the simultaneous offering and refusal of pregnant meaning. Once again Theodor Adorno—the lyric is the "Sonnenuhr der Zeit"[3]—makes his strategy heard: to go for the immanent self-account that emerges from the text. And it is this: the self is easy in a soul-house, nature, which nevertheless insists on its harshness toward us. Snyder has himself translated our inner-voice tones, stapling us to his reading—of a moment hungry for wholeness, making do temporarily with a nature that is the most trustworthy available *kosmos*.

What about the whole-world roundness move that we took in the effort to know Kuaua? Need we this kind of mediation, on our way to a nearly contemporary text like Snyder's? The answer is *yes,* we do. Time eats discourse hungrily. (Time eats my sentence as it leaves my mouth.) Time—can we not define it as shed existence soliciting order? Snyder's text lies "backward" into the history of its language, into—for example—a Wordsworth we can neither expunge nor settle for; and "forward" into our continuing preoccupation, to find existence-zones we belong to. That "forward" meets and is defined by the immediate "backward" of our awareness, as we write today against threats seemingly less predictable and more deadly than those Snyder's poem pawed back.

Translation, then, is required for the reading of "A Walk." The threshold posed to our backward-seeking consciousness will yield, but not to the first glance, not to button-touch. In one sense, "le poème se fait de mots, pas d'idées," but the words in question— even in this poem—are so historically charged that they evoke with them a network of connotations that are integral parts of their meaning and that must be read against their own implicit horizon as well as against that of their reader. In this sense, the sites of Kuaua and "A Walk" require both prepared and goal-directed interpretation.

By pure whim we move our *musée imaginaire* backward in time, and turn the corner into Alfred de Vigny's "La Mort du Loup."[4] By the clock we have retreated 114 years from the slippery

and vanishing point of the Snyder present; but what in fact is
pastness in this "backwards"-moving inquiry?

Start where the question is tangible, with "backwards." I have
argued at length—in *The Fact of Literature*[5]—for the propriety of
thinking about the past from the position of the present and for
applying that method and perspective to curricular changes in
universities. "Backwards" thinking, in that context, meant gradual
penetration of the layers of creation and causation that had presented you with your "I"; penetration from more to less recent.
But to what does this spatial metaphor of "backward" point in the
object studied? Is "backward-standing" visible in the object, in
Kuaua itself, or in Snyder's poem? Is "pastness" visible or knowable
there?

It is hard to imagine a trait, in Snyder's "A Walk" or Alfred
de Vigny's "La Mort du Loup," which we would call *pastness*. We
could refer to a whole set of resistances against our immediate
understanding, which express themselves in the form and argument
of that poem. (Even that notion, *resistances,* appears to prejudice
the inquiry—implying that time must progressively wear down
meaning—and yet for now we can go carefully with that perspective.) Resistances of that kind will constitute the threshold to be
coped with and crossed. What increment of resistance—over Snyder's poem—is presented by "La Mort du Loup"?

La Mort du Loup

I

LES nuages couraient sur la lune enflammée
Comme sur l'incendie on voit fuir la fumée,
Et les bois étaient noirs jusques à l'horizon.
Nous marchions, sans parler, dans l'humide gazon,
Dans la bruyère épaisse et dans les hautes brandes,
Lorsque, sous des sapins pareils à ceux des Landes,
Nous avons aperçu les grands ongles marqués
Par les loups voyageurs que nous avions traqués.
Nous avons écouté, retenant notre haleine
Et le pas suspendu.—Ni le bois ni la plaine
Ne poussaient un soupir dans les airs; seulement
La girouette en deuil criait au firmament;

Car le vent, élevé bien au-dessus des terres,
N'effleurait de ses pieds que les tours solitaires,
Et les chênes d'en bas, contre les rocs penchés,
Sur leurs coudes semblaient endormis et couchés.
Rien ne bruissait donc, lorsque, baissant la tête,
Le plus vieux des chasseurs qui s'étaient mis en quête
A regardé le sable en s'y couchant; bientôt,
Lui que jamais ici l'on ne vit en défaut,
A déclaré tout bas que ces marques récentes
Annonçaient la démarche et les griffes puissantes
De deux grands loups-cerviers et de deux louveteaux.
Nous avons tous alors préparé nos couteaux,
Et, cachant nos fusils et leurs lueurs trop blanches,
Nous allions pas à pas en écartant les branches.
Trois s'arrêtent, et moi, cherchant ce qu'ils voyaient,
J'aperçois tout à coup deux yeux qui flamboyaient,
Et je vois au delà quatre formes légères
Qui dansaient sous la lune au milieu des bruyères,
Comme font chaque jour, à grand bruit sous nos yeux,
Quand le maître revient, les lévriers joyeux.
Leur forme était semblable et semblable la danse;
Mais les enfants du Loup se jouaient en silence,
Sachant bien qu'à deux pas, ne dormant qu'à demi,
Se couche dans ses murs l'homme, leur ennemi.
Le père était debout, et plus loin, contre un arbre,
Sa louve reposait comme celle de marbre
Qu'adoraient les Romains et dont les flancs velus
Couvaient les demi-dieux Rémus et Romulus.
Le Loup vient et s'assied, les deux jambes dressées,
Par leurs ongles crochus dans le sable enfoncées.
Il s'est jugé perdu, puisqu'il était surpris,
Sa retraite coupée et tous ses chemins pris;
Alors il a saisi, dans sa gueule brûlante,
Du chien le plus hardi la gorge pantelante,
Et n'a pas desserré ses mâchoires de fer,
Malgré nos coups de feu, qui traversaient sa chair,
Et nos couteaux aigus qui, comme des tenailles,
Se croisaient en plongeant dans ses larges entrailles,
Jusqu'au dernier moment où le chien étranglé,
Mort longtemps avant lui, sous ses pieds a roulé.
Le Loup le quitte alors et puis il nous regarde.
Les couteaux lui restaient au flanc jusqu'à la garde,
Le clouaient au gazon tout baigné dans son sang;
Nos fusils l'entouraient en sinistre croissant.
Il nous regarde encore, ensuite il se recouche,

Tout en léchant le sang répandu sur sa bouche,
Et, sans daigner savoir comment il a péri,
Refermant ses grands yeux, meurt sans jeter un cri.

II

J'ai reposé mon front sur mon fusil sans poudre,
Me prenant à penser, et n'ai pu me résoudre
A poursuivre sa Louve et ses fils, qui, tous trois,
Avaient voulu l'attendre, et, comme je le crois,
Sans des deux louveteaux, la belle et, sombre veuve
Ne l'eût pas laissé seul subir la grande épreuve;
Mais son devoir était de les sauver, afin
De pouvoir leur apprendre à bien souffrir la faim,
A ne jamais entrer dans le pacte des villes
Que l'homme a fait avec les animaux serviles
Qui chassent devant lui, pour avoir le coucher,
Les premiers possesseurs du bois et du rocher.

III

Hélas! ai-je pensé, malgré ce grand nom d'Hommes,
Que j'ai honte de nous, débiles que nous sommes!
Comment on doit quitter la vie et tous ses maux,
C'est vous qui le savez, sublimes animaux!
A voir ce que l'on fut sur terre et ce qu'on laisse,
Seul le silence est grand; tout le reste est faiblesse.
—Ah! je t'ai bien compris, sauvage voyageur,
Et ton dernier regard m'est allé jusqu'au coeur!
Il disait: "Si tu peux, fais que ton âme arrive,
A force de rester studieuse et pensive,
Jusqu'à ce haut degré de stoïque fierté
Où, naissant dans les bois, j'ai tout d'abord monté.
Gémir, pleurer, prier, est également lâche.
Fais énergiquement ta longue et lourde tâche
Dans la voie où le sort a voulu t'appeler,
Puis, après, comme moi, souffre et meurs sans parler."

Resistance flies at us. Make your own anthology of texts that reflect on man's inferiorities to the more natural world. I turn to Robinson Jeffers—"I'd sooner kill a man than a hawk / if it weren't for the penalties"—or Tennyson's "flower in the crannied wall" and begin constructing. From the outset I identify—without perhaps understanding—what flavors Vigny's resistance. He doesn't recommend the wisdom of nature. He requires of man a harsh

view of his own life—his "longue et lourde tâche"—then a merely
enduring silence, as death disregardingly puts him away. Resistance
this is—compared with the kind of abrasiveness Snyder feels out
in the nature of "A Walk." Snyder's nature refuses itself any sentiment, but refuses to deny all value to the human *tâche*. Vigny's
resistance is equally apparent if we contrast the perspective in Jeffers
or Tennyson, both of whom we can reach with our present voices.
Tennyson—of a century with Vigny—works his variation on that
pantheism which is part of *philosophia perennis,* which causes little
agony to our contemporary, late-hippie sensibilities. Jeffers is the
classic *désenchanté du monde humain,* loving what he (against his
better knowledge) knows is nature's indifference. Neither his nor
Tennyson's perspective gives us that "mort du Loup" sense that
we here rub our minds on a darkly grinding otherness. We are
used, at worst, to that man-indifferent nature of W. T. Stace,
Bertrand Russell, or Joseph Krutch, which provokes a bleak (or
even flamboyant) heroism in us.

Vigny's language surrounds and determines the resistance he
makes of himself. (Text-language is history, perhaps the most tangible trace of man's temporality. Derrida plays loose with this
precious thread of continuity when—say, in his essay, "Writing,
Sign, and Play"—he attacks the integrity and persistence of the
written text.) Snyder showed his mastery of colloquial language,
our turn of sound; he doctored speech with a skill that made it
seem more natural than nature. Vigny rhymes alexandrines with
the cumulative effect—here the reason for my long citation—of
elegant remorselessness, the power of always slightly postponed
insistence, of dreadful *souffle.* The starkness of his message—*"gémir,
pleurer, prier, est également lâche"*—is perfectly hewn to the ham-
mering of itself in; forever closing on the amplitude of its couplets,
miming completeness, then opening again wide enough—note the
hungry enjambment—onto the jaws of a new finality.

Prosodic vehicle and argument twin up here in a rare challenging. Reading this poem today from our sliding present means
bouncing our voice off walls truly constructible only in a *musée
imaginaire.* Knowing who built these walls—a Vigny embittered
by a bumbling Revolutionary era, personal crises unending and
savage, and the perplexities of his *âme immortelle* trapped by sci-

entific materialism—knowing who thus built is to understand even more deeply than Vigny's text lets out about itself what a threshold "La Mort" must be for us.

Are resistances traces of pastness? The way through this argument could get out of hand, and yet it is on our way. Textural resistances are in themselves no proof of ancient withdrawal. (What texts resist us more than *Finnegans Wake* or *Hérodiade,* which are relatively ours?) However, resistances fostered by broad historical parameters, such as we meet in "La Mort du Loup," are as true indicators as we may find of the signature of time on language. Whole-world roundness in which we meet ourselves as past still arches over us from Vigny's historical embeddedness, a rainbow of continuity to the far source of which we reach—through Vigny as text—somewhere in the world that sprang him loose, early nineteenth-century despair, a Revolution going flat, and that inner demystification to which Jouffroy dedicated juicy *angoisse.*

Jumping "backward" from Vigny—and in the "jump" we see just where the arbitrary enters in constructing and finding cultural history—we land in an earlier century, and pick a name: Angelus Silesius, first half of the seventeenth. In so doing, we Westerners retreat through one of our great Maginot lines, behind which the past conceals secrets. We move through an eighteenth century transition that is pulling down the ebullient facades of Romanticism—poets as unacknowledged legislators of the world—into that seventeenth century mind-world which inevitably, still, whiffs of the medieval. Try out Addison and Steele again, for that familiar essay-tone, or Lessing, or—of course—Diderot; how can you not hear your inner voice's immediate echo? The past as yourself is all over you. But push a little farther into the line. How about Mme. de Lafayette or Winckelmann or Dryden? Does the hearing aid still work? There is increasing static and confusion, for which—here we palp with the myths we need—we must blame an older assumption about personality. For the three authors mentioned, the author-artist is a formal maker of formal personae and thoughts, a ritualist of the imagination we may have needed our own late century to value properly. Angelus Silesius takes us both more and less sharply into that ritual prehistory. (The perplexities of all historical linearity! Woe to the rectangular reestablisher!) Less sharply, oddly enough, because with this direct speaker to God we enter a narrow, brightly lit place interior to each of us. More sharply though, because the space in question is one we are unused to occupying. But more than unused! In occupying that space we easily—Thomas Merton, Alan Watts, hippies united—fool ourselves with a sentimental hollowing of quietude. We deceive ourselves with a personal and presumably direct access to the bitter, extravagant, and paradox-shot-through mode of

> Auch könnte nur der Herz zu einer Krippe werden,
> Gott würde noch einmal ein Kind auf dieser Erden.

or

> Die Schönheit ist ein Licht; je mehr dir Licht gebricht,
> Je greulicher du auch an Leib und Seele bist.

or

> Nichts dünkt mich hoch zu sein: ich bin das höchste Ding,
> Weil auch Gott ohne mich ihm selber ist gering.[6]

Can we go farther toward naming what it is we can barely name here? The form—the shape, mode—is that same alexandrine on which I expatiated with Vigny. But Silesius—whose work is contemporary with Corneille's—hammers a far tighter parcel than Vigny, whose remorselessness belongs always to what he has not yet said. It is not just that Silesius is an epigrammatist but that his whole sensibility, proposal then paradoxical clarification, compels him to that form. Nothing about Silesius' epigrams refers beyond itself, though their reference back in contains the "world in a grain of sand."

Silesius' themes are simple (though constantly self-criticizing, upside-downing)—and illustratable through almost any random pick. (If in fact he composed the first three hundred of these radiators in four days, we can imagine the white flame of intensity that must work through them.) The theological paradox at the center is simple to state though hard to feel from the inside: *mundus pulcherrimum nihil,* the world is a gorgeous nothing. In the "gorgeous" rest those leaping virtues Silesius finds in the *mundus,* the created world: its beauty, its potential for love, its architectural order, its centering on man—"das höchste Ding"—in whom the mystery of all creation boils, that image of God without which God is not himself. The first and last citations, above, bear on this point and stand for subtle woven variations through hundreds of epigrams. The second quotation, in paradoxical praise of that beauty which makes all that is unbeautiful uglier, helps us across the (always nearby) bridge from the world's beauty to its vanity, its *nihil.* Nothingness, here, is the instant passing of a bauble, a perception of passing common in some form, and at some time, to all religious world-grasps. For Silesius the *nihil* of the world and the plentitude of its Creator constantly interconvert, the one growing—and reinforcing the other—as the other diminishes.

Eggs with apples it may be, yet we must compare Silesius' argument with those of Vigny and Snyder—if we want to measure time, if we want to set our threshold's high-jump bar. Snyder and Vigny both place us, through their narrators, in a *mundus;* do so by a language tone, and by a reference into nature. For all their differences—sufficient for us to read major resistances into "La Mort du Loup"—these two sensibilities take nature as man's large field of dialectical self-discovery. In turning that way they interest themselves in what is their good, their human saving and in the talk of their times as modes of imitating that saving. Silesius imitates the conversation of soul with God, in its concern with—among other things—nature and beauty. But nature itself—the created, the *pulcherrimum nihil*—hardly provokes his finesse, except in the exquisite form of the alexandrine epigram. In this discourse with God Silesius most convinces us—not that God is dead but that we have forgotten how to say that God is alive.

Round-world perspectives? The Silesian Angel becomes himself from a tradition—Eckehart, Taüler, Böhme—intimate to him, so close that he can ring delicate changes on it by a fillip of syntax. Looking forward, for Silesius, can only mean looking into the Lap of God, yet in his forward our orientation toward a past—an eternal past—meets him. The world readored by Heidegger, Snyder, Alan Watt, Simone Weil, Charles Williams is once again a world in which we can at least rediscover the *sursum corda,* the strange joyous silence at the center of things. Our century bled of nineteenth-century optimism is precisely the locale for rediscovering a genuine optimism. If we go that route we admit that the Silesius threshold is no deeper in us, no harder to find and cross, than the Vigny threshold. Once we lean into this wind, though, we need to remember much more than was said above about the pitfalls awaiting when we feel easy with ancient religious paradox.

Driving the fuse into a remoter past—from Vigny to Silesius—is not certain to increase the difficulty of threshold crossing. Places in the distant past may be brightly lighted, and those nearby muddy to vision—like the uncorrected onset of presbyopia. (Though we have again to add that there is no guarantee for the accuracy or fullness of this retrospection, outside the better and continued doing of the retrospection itself. Threshold crossing is not more or less than what it is.) Furthermore, this interior inquiry, by which we struggle toward an adequacy toward our whole selves, takes place under the sign of the Primal, White Light itself.

What are we seeking as we plunge backward except the Great Forward, origin and impulse toward the construction of art and, beyond that, of the entire fictive enterprise by which our species' own last testament is written? What indeed, except, farther back yet than Kuaua or Altemira, or even than Golding's or Vardis Fisher's inheritors, the first germ plasm of the organic? (I will not allude, though I long to, to that bridge from the organic back, that threshold to the inorganic over which we can walk across lichen-backed escarpments into our preconscious and stand as close as a planet to God. I can say that the simple mention of this antiquity proves something: that in casting farther back into ourselves we close passionately with what is essential in us as our history and that in the proximity of that Primal we are close as we can get to what we will become.)

The *bateau ivre* of our backwards consciousness has already brushed a mystery, finding itself more comfortably harbored with Silesius than with Vigny. Thus the voice-criterion proves complex for we can on occasion hear ourselves, catch our own intelligible accent, in a past far more distant than we should imagine available.

Kuaua was an initial instance, and now Silesius has been advanced as another. While on the other hand a writer like Alfred de Vigny, on our side of epochal Revolutions and scientific discoveries, may on important issues convert himself (for us now) from a threshold into a roadblock. All such unexpectedness, of course, will hardly have surprised any except the clock linearists, usually today disguised as Marxists hoping that time's and reason's unfoldings correspond. But if the surprises are slight—for most of us—the implications of them can never be taken for granted. Interpenetrating psyches, ranged at widely separate points in history, seem to meet at holes they punch into the sky, seem to stand for the Platonic lobby—such as we can allow it today.

The case of François Villon, like that of Silesius, will present us with our own faces in the mirror, but with a million cautions— as when we truly look at ourselves in glass—against assuming we can read what we see there. We return to the tone of Kuaua, and listen with our souls to

> Item, mon corps j'ordonne et laisse
> A nostre grant mere la terre;
> Les vers n'y trouveront grant gresse
> Trop lui a fait fain dure guerre.
> Or lui soit delivré grant erre,
> De terre vint, en terre tourne.
> Toute chose, se par trop n'erre,
> Voulentiers en son lieu retourne.[7]

Villon's *Testament* has given away many a real and mock good, to friend and enemy, but the item above exceeds them all in directness. I attend to its simple turns because they mesh back into the soul-nature-salvation dialogue that has forced itself up through our previous texts.

Growth-points are few here. What seasons the piece except waxing and waning? (Its large whole—the ashes to ashes—is evident and of its time, and of our time.) I "leave my body" but it is at the same time "willing" to return to the earth; a pinch of irony. What "I" give furthermore is skinny, if willing, a detail hard to ignore in rewriting or rethinking the poem. The balance sheet of this Villon seasoning is a worldview at a bias to any we have aligned.

Nature—this time—is the hungry grandmother ready for a nip at her returning offspring. (The "nature" of Snyder, Vigny, or Silesius is nowhere audible here, in this lusty *memento mori physis* of a premodern gaillard.) The "I"—soul, poet, narrator—is textural and spatiotemporal, like the "I" of Snyder's poem and in fact here guarantees as it does throughout Villon that intimacy his poetic legacy has consistently found in him. Villon's "I"—in this poem—pretends no interest in its salvation, except through writing about that lack of interest. On this point his time's Catholic telism simply takes over, divides body from soul and promises the latter a bliss not even worm-bleakness can dim.

All this adds up to specific issues—and a general point. One of the issues asserts itself to the neglect of others; and the general point wants to come first.

What kind of problem does Villon's text present, that it can be penetrated to such a point of analysis as mine? All seems so wrapped up here, the threshold so clearly outlined and crossable! The far side of it from us, already so present! All has been rapidly entered, relations to later texts apportioned, and yet style-texture has been ignored. That is the problem.

To work at that texture-problem I turn to certain translations of Villon into English, from which we can perhaps discover what we cannot say of him, and in that negative manner isolate what is there in difference from us. (For if poetry is what gets lost in translation, this losing effort is a unique means of finding out what poetry is.)

To press the experiment I begin with a prose crib that pretends to nothing. (But something about that needs explaining!) Wyndham Lewis—simply to be useful to the reader of his Villon biography—puts,

> Item. I give and bequeath my body to the Earth, our common Mother. The worms will not find much meat on it, for hunger has bitten it too near the bone already. Let it be delivered as soon as it may be: of earth it was made, to earth it returns. Everything, unless I err, goes willingly back to the place whence it came.

Since first we read our Caesar (or Racine, or Madach, or D'Annunzio) we have brushed literal cribs and in general, I suspect, with a rather rigid sense of what they are. (*Guides to meaning* we will have called them.) The fact is, the threshold Villon becomes is not even found here, let alone crossed. How can dead words guide us to the life inside a text? No part of a text that has come to life is untouched by its transformed spirit. What about Lepper's?

> Item, my body's carrion
> I leave to our great mother *Earth;*
> The worms will not wax fat thereon,
> For famine has reduced my girth.
> Make haste: from dust it drew its birth
> And unto dust it shall return.
> Each thing its proper place with mirth
> Regaineth, as the wise discern.

This time, rhyme and meter have, as they say, been preserved, and to that extent—on a surface level—the original has been resaid. But the sayability criterion for translations is difficult to apply. Poets and philosophers return at intervals to the healthy admonition that we should say or speak our thoughts out before us, to hear us. While riding in a car, Allen Ginsburg composes an epic of America into a tape recorder so that he can listen to and modify his voice. Why shouldn't we transplant these admonitions into advice to the reader, the recapturer of (say) past texts? Against the voice box of the soul, or the air wall of our milieu, we should be able to feel comfortable resaying the text. It should be in our voice. We vomit internally on Lepper's last two lines, which pad when unnecessary, which import a trivial and inappropriate sentiment. The cruxes are barely looked at here, and no growth-point is given attention. Translators of this stamp cross thresholds before finding out how deeply the simple in Villon baffles us.

> Item: I bequeath and leave my flesh
> and bones to our great mother, earth.
> The worms won't find it full or fresh
> for hunger pinched its pennyworth.
> Dispose it soon in its last berth.
> From earth it yearned, to earth must yield.
> Things always find their place on earth
> if they don't wander far afield.

Villon's simple *toute chose,* which "wills" its way back to its place, bedevils our rhyme; though with no excusing of "if they don't wander far afield." Once again, with Dale as with Lepper and Wyndham Lewis' bounceless pony, we will have to conclude that the translator's incompetence argues his failure in threshold crossing. To be blunt: none of these three authors gives promise of knowing where Villon's text is. They flail toward Villon in an English that is neither prose nor art.

I stress translation for a change, in Villon's case, because I believe that the act of translation is intimately critical, is perhaps the decisive criterion of understanding. No work of historical comprehension demands more than translation, in the way of detailed tone hearing, larger sensibility organization, and plain conceptual adequacy.

Atop these translations—which are far from the best I can find and are chosen for that reason—I place an effort, one voice I find in my body, to define Villon as threshold and to cross him:

> Now this: muh body.
> Ah turns it over to Ma Earth, Ma Mudder,
> Fastfood thinpickings worm-fodder
> (Ahm a six foot two intestine).
> Special Duhlivery ah've scribbled on this corpus
> And slipped muhself back into a mail-slot in the humus.
> "Warn't a moment of resistance.
> Ah knows muh place."

The gaillard tone failing me and being the rarest of mastery in our time, I slunk toward the characterful imp of dialect. (Pursued, as I have noted, by the belief that what I can understand will be what I can say, what I can put out before me without discovering the *je* has truly become an *other*.) Pound used such dialect in his "Old Marse Shao" translation from Confucius, to sustain a historical (just postbellum) mood. Today—a Civil Rights war away from Pound—black dialect comes to me as a reach for what ironic bravura "Auschwitz" has left to us. (Augie March, where are you under the high-tech rain?) Wrong I may be—in my translation tactic or assessment of our moment. But right I am, on the matter of era-tone and ear-responsibility. We must—and that gives us latitude—say our translation in the breath reserved for us by our moment.

Have I penetrated to the far side of Villon? What I *can* say— that I can say this translation without blushing—will be only as good as the evidential coin I can back it with. I will need to show that my reading of Villon makes his own poem better for us, richer with human content and human difference, and that both threshold of experience and sense of transcendence fit themselves to Villon's poem-body as it works up through us. Whether I succeed or not— quite apart from my claims—is not for me to decide, for I simply introduce criteria for success, for anyone's success in working back into the past. This is the round-world criterion, dressed in rigorous language-weeds.

Has the past's threshold raised its crossbar with each move we have made? Snyder, Vigny, Silesius, Villon? I have already pointed—rather complexly—to some kinds of *yes* or *no* with which to answer this question. In some sense, certainly, Villon's mournful-hearty consignment of his body, his *homo viator* marginalism, are part of the pre-Renaissance perspective. To that extent the translation of him—penetration and use of him in act—least permits us easy access. We are puzzled whether to sleep on our feet (Wyndham Lewis) or stand on our heads (Will). We are touching the backs of our minds.

What I introduce next—as the last two pieces of evidence— will, like Kuaua, raise the question of who we are, will take us to one set of limits and force from us either the password or a tremulous *je rends*. I speak of our honored-ignored culture-mother, Greco-Roman antiquity.

Having logged fifteen years as a "professional" classicist, and repeatedly taught "lit in trans"—Homer to Aulus Gellius—I draw my scars as testimony: the Greco-Roman world, as a whole, is harder for us to read than Ancient China and far harder than Ancient Mexico. Yet when it comes to cases—this text, that sculpture—we can recover a sense of kinship to us which a random Ganesha, Chacmool, or Avalokitesvara will rarely reinforce. I speak Western ashamedly, for Westerners.

Horace and Sappho, then—extremes, foreigners, friends. Thresholds our immediate ancestors crossed in their way up to the time of our birth, to our first word *bread,* not *bekos* or *panis*.

Horace first, where he touches the mortality and salvation themes:

> Te maris et terrae numeroque carentis harenae
>   mensorem cohibent, Archyta,
> pulveris exigui prope litus parva Matinum
>   munera, nec quicquam tibi prodest
>
> aërias temptasse domos animoque rotundum
>   percurrisse polum morituro.
> occidit et Pelopis genitor, conviva deorum,
>   Tithonusque remotus in auras,
>
> et Iovis arcanis Minos admissus, habentque
>   Tartara Panthoiden iterum Orco
> demissum, quamvis clipeo Troiana refixo
>   tempora testatus nihil ultra
>
> nervos atque cutem morti concesserat atrae,
>   iudice te non sordidus auctor
> naturae verique. sed omnis una manet nox,
>   et calcanda semel via leti.
>
> dant alios Furiae torvo spectacula Marti;
>   exitio est avidum mare nautis;
> mixta senum ac iuvenum densentur funera; nullum
>   saeva caput Proserpina fugit.[8]

Thou, Archytas, measurer of the sea and land and countless sands, art confined in a small mound of paltry earth near the Matinian shore; nor doth it aught avail thee that thou didst once explore the gods' ethereal homes and didst traverse in thought the circling vault of heaven. For thou wast born to die! Death befell also Pelops' sire, though once he sat at the table of the gods; Tithonus, too, translated to the skies, and Minos, partner of Jove's own secrets; and Tartarus holds the son of Panthous, sent down a second time to Orcus, though by taking down the shield he bore witness to Trojan times, and yielded to black Death naught but his sinews and his frame,—to thy mind no common judge of Nature and of truth.

But a common night awaiteth every man, and Death's path must be trodden once for all. Some, the Furies offer as a sight for cruel Mars; the hungry sea is the sailor's ruin. Without distinction the deaths of old and young follow close on each other's heels; cruel Proserpine spares no head.

Nature is present as Death, quite simply; and as such without aperture or growth-points. (In Snyder, nature was distant and rough but not lethal; in Vigny she was unsentimental and stoic, yet capable of provoking dignity; even in Villon, nature was a comfortable fit, wormy but congenial to the cosmic.) Horace's nature as death is without attitude or character, simply snuffs out. As such it is that ancient other, like the sea which—to fifth-century Athenians—seemed nonhuman, though they posted Poseidon on it to remind themselves of its personal anger.

Horace blinds death with art—more antiquity. (Auden, whose favorite reading included Cochrane's *From Christianity to Classical Culture,* knew what an evening out, what a regressive sanity, belongs even to the immediate pre-Christian years; what *Latina aurea* truly meant as shimmering metal before a blinded and fearful Augustine.)

> Te maris et terrae numeroque carentis harenae
>   mensorem cohibent, Archyta,
> pulveris exigui prope litus parva Matinum
>   munera

Why should not Augustine—in his discovery of the accent and bias in death—have dreaded Horace's serene yielding in language that negates yielding? Death, Horace says, is so indifferently rigorous that it fits in a small pocket—*pulveris exigui*—that it can easily accommodate the greatest minds of an age. Horace's brilliant formulation of death's brilliant formula brings the existential to a standstill. "Le buste"—this kind of "buste"—truly "survit à la cité."

What threshold is this? Indifference is here the problem, antiquity itself, and not an easy problem for the Christian era. Christianity—and the gradually constructed threshold that means it—punched an angular hole into history and the interpretation of it, forever relieving *tò ón* of its antique geometrism. To believe because it is absurd would have to have seemed—to Horace, Aristotle, or Thucydides—full-moon insanity. Such in-difference, hewn out of architectural syntax, becomes itself a text as sturdy as death.

Crossing backward over such a threshold presents us with those increasing tone difficulties that are Classical Antiquity (which are the source, where it works, of that Ben or Sam Johnson muscularity that justifies our entire bumbled classical tradition). Some of the reasons for this difficulty have been intimated, and others could be added—such as the mixing of the highest soundcraft with the bluntest semantics:

> sed omnis una manet nox
> et calcanda semel via leti.

The historical or round-world problem enters here too. Much time elapses between the earliest *medium aevum* that we can hear—Chaucer, perhaps Alfred, Hroswitha—and even the latest Classic—perhaps Ausonius; and, at that, these extremes are almost off the available voice register. Yet in those intervening centuries there are changes deep enough to alienate us from ourselves. (Of course Kuaua—or Les Eyzies or Angkor Wat—lie farther from us than Horace, lie beyond more distant time or culture barriers; but in their starkly existential presence, over against us, they force us to topple our weight against them. Horace, by contrast, is a tight filigree resistance. That resistance is the sign of pastness on Horace, a sign both inherent and accidental in his poem, for to Sappho it would have been only the potentiality of a way of looking and feeling.)

The lure of an intelligible cultural history is sacrificed in the perspective of this essay, as it would have to be in a comparative literature (or culture) explicated from present to past. We are moving backward and encountering signatures of resistance that are on the whole—but with many tufty qualifications—harder to read the farther we go. The qualifications—as in the jump from Silesius to Villon—thwart order and process. But such forms of intelligibility are anyway suspect, for they are too easily tempted to lead all history to the threshold of a particular meaning, our moment. (Hegel and Spengler, as well as Erich Voegelin and Herbert Muller in *The Uses of the Past,* will do for examples of this temptation.) Above all it—this past-to-present causal perspective—obscures a double actuality: that such developmental *an-angke* advances by whim, accident, and at the will of the influenced; and—a corollary to the latter—that the influenced element, the text of Goethe or Joyce, gives the past its power to effect, takes to itself the power to free meaning from time. The perspective of our present essay lures with other metaphors and rewards—as I have argued in an essay, "The Fact of Literature." The dominant metaphor here will be "reconquering," "taking back terrain from or within ourselves," "recovering our whole map." As our emphasis will be on recuperation, the sought reward will be a kind of salvation—equality to oneself. Threshold crossing, consequently, will be an unending effort to reach one's totality.

Sappho will lure us to the final way station on the example-journey of this essay. With a glance at her work—which stands inside the last language pliable to this wayfarer—we can force ourselves back to textuality.

Five centuries separate Horace from Sappho—and immeasurable political-social change. (From Snyder to Villon, I suppose, is a far less tumultuous transformation than the one before us.) Yet some time-unity clings to the lyric achievement of those centuries—and cuts them off, presses us by contrast to note the consanguinity of our Villon-to-Snyder poetic continuum. One piece of Sappho may hint at this point, while forcing our thematic material back to a wall:

> Hesperos, you bring home all the bright dawn disperses,
> bring home the sheep,
> bring home the goat, bring the child home to its mother.[9]

We have run at our texts—and at the Kuaua experience—with many different weapons. I began—and will conclude—this essay by stressing a spatiotemporal hallowing required before taking up the past, a past lying within us but far under our surfaces. That historical self-readying proved part of cognition as well as of askesis, and promoted the round-world methodology. I meant that the past artwork took up into it what was its past, and took that up against, or into, an horizon which was that work's telos, what that work wanted to become in some auditor or reader-to-be. At the same time the reader—of Silesius or Sappho—read against his past and future, made of himself as global a consciousness-arc as he could, and in that extension of self worked to intersect with the past work's arc. The intersections achieved this way would be points of recuperation of what is never inherently past. In the course of practicing this cognitive method we found our poetic texts on the whole, with many slippages and startlings, receding from us as their present.

Each way-step toward the receding horizon has been a threshold, a *limen* to cross and understand from its far, as well as its near, side. (At the end of this receding line lay the other sequences, like that leading from the organic back to the inorganic over the lichen bridge. Thresholds kept popping up like ducks in a shooting gallery, yielding at last—as in Samuel Alexander's *Space, Time, and Deity*—to God, the ultimate threshold, beyond whom—if one were to go so far—oneself would perhaps appear as old and as new as the Dawn.) Thresholds had seemed barriers worth attending to, for they represented points at which consciousness was revved to its highest peak of articulation and intelligence.

Passing across these thresholds—as it happens and as it returns us to Sappho—we have run down a narrow line of themes. Death, nature, and salvation (or coping response) have lain across each of our texts. Various points have been made, but one especially clears the path into Sappho. Horace shines with a pagan clarity or—if you prefer—is dark with the uncomplexly pre-Christian light. For him, both death and art are absolutes and to a finality we can conceive but probably not feel. (So deeply has the Christian or theist possibility touched our age largely unequipped for the death-threshold.) The result is a species of secular sadness that we find surprising in the ebullient ancient lyric—in Catullus, Pindar, Archilochos, and Sappho. Sappho's fragment, above, crumbles off precisely that sadness. The first feel of it is imagist, word-pictures of Evening, the pastoral folding up into itself (a Fragonard or Turner landscape). The first line closes, with Dusk, over what Dawn had dispersed; perfect symmetry biased only by the direct address—which is to Dusk, not Dawn. (Right here in the quiet beauty of the cyclical, Sappho touches a sensibility knowably not ours.) Nature's quiet fertilities are pulled back in by the croupier hook of rest, as is the very setting-out in nature, the child who returns to the womb. Sappho's light dust of sadness matches Horace's gorgeous yielding to fatality, challenging us all the more, perhaps, for its refusal to insist. We can measure this delicate Sapphic resistance by contrasting it to the opener, more salvation-implying nature modes Vigny, Snyder, or even Villon offer in words. The point of this contrast is fine. Vigny and Villon, after all, sing man a dark song. And at that we could have turned almost anywhere—in Beckett, in Céline, in Nietzsche—to recent texts less philosophically consoling than Vigny's. The positive in all these songs would have lain precisely in their refusal of resignation. The finitude and disquiet of the human condition would in these more recent authors be something to fight. In Horace and Sappho the *nox una* would be acceptable, might readily be converted into the deadly beauty of song. Keats' "Ode to a Grecian Urn" reminds us how nearly, yet only wistfully, we can at our most liquid aspire to the limpid vision of the classical lyric.

The threshold of the Greco-Roman lyric is not the highest. (Selections from the Vedas or the *Book of Songs* might have smashed us against indifferences unimagined, more perplexing than the Horatian-Sapphic balance of death with beauty.) We have not gone for high drama in the historical-literary thresholding of this essay, though by opening with Kuaua I meant to press my eyes at least once against a culture-frontier. I meant to put forth one example that exercised all our capacities of resistance overcoming. Even Sappho, distant and still, cannot have exercised us so greatly.

Two conclusions force themselves on this chapter.

One—the practical—clambers out mandatory. To a surprising degree, the older the text—or artwork or musical composition—the more available it may seem to be. Sappho and Confucius and Lao Tzu and the *Popol Vuh* will inevitably seem, in this sense, to be low-threshold obstacles. We will read those texts against a relatively little documented or understood background. We will

go swiftly, all too swiftly, into those texts. (About sixth-century-
B.C. Lesbos we know little, while first-century-B.C. Rome, Horace's
Rome, is almost as heavily documented as the nineteenth century
of our era.) For this reason, I realize, I may conclude too easily
about Sappho's availability. We do, of course, find that repeated
readings of her grow increasingly comfortable. Her texts confirm
our instinct that we "know what she is talking about." (How
differently, in this, from the effect of relatively recent text makers
like Louise Labé or Maurice Scève.) However, there are different
species of difficulty, and a distinction is in order. Sappho is not
hard to read—but to understand. Kuaua is not hard to code-
decipher, but profoundly difficult to be inside of.

My second conclusion returns to the larger question, Of what
value is the search for our receding historical thresholds? The
instance of Sappho will bear on us again. Her text is easy syntactically and imagistically, as are the other texts we have dealt with.
But her text is hard too, making simple space in which to carve out
a perspective that is limpidly not ours; and in this sense her text is
at a far reach from us, farther—by far—than a document like
Vigny's, which on its face has the look of another world. Sappho's
kind of difficulty, deceptive as it is, suggests the value a mind-
threshold presents to us, forcing us into and through onto the far
side of itself. We have looked at several such loving obstacles in
artistic language, as they presented themselves to both translation
and interpretation. We have dealt with art as the threshold through
which nature passes on its journey to form. And we have watched
both critical methods and species of language at work, differen-
tiating themselves and intersecting through one another as mutually posed thresholds. Thresholds were at each point zones of
high organizational value, in which our knowledge and experience
were coordinated.

Locating our historical thresholds is mapping our inner territory temporally, thus finding where we are—as knowing and
feeling beings. Locating those thresholds out from the present is
archaeology of the self, in part determining where and what we
now are by exploring our origins—with the purpose of reincor-
porating them. In this archaeology thresholds are points at which,
in accepting increasing distances within ourselves, we encounter

unprepared depths. Depths? Yes, on that advanced metaphor, lying athwart our hitherto architectural imagery, let us pull this essay back into itself.

That testifying by which we make known that we have met and are crossing a threshold of consciousness, is the cry or incision-mark elicited by transition-experience. (The next and last essay will be devoted to the sound of that cry.) We enter a fresh depth when we go back, or go in, to Snyder's experience of us, or Silesius', or Horace's. The inward serial alignment of these texts, by and large on a scale of increasing resistances, guarantees to such texts a cumulative depth as one palimpsest layer above another enforces the thick code-web of the past over the present. But the threshold is truly a sill or barrier behind which the riches of harvest are stored. The depth of the land is there.

In the difficult text I translate, in the marble face I carve, in the tissue of assembled water-accounts, in the effort to read great Silver Latin poetry: in all these aesthetic struggles I come on fresh and demanding new-old forms of myself, for which I must find internal interpretation-keys. The depths I enter surprise me—for I had no way but them to discover how unknown I was to myself—but at the same time reassure, as does a long journey home. The value of rediscovering these depth-centers is plain enough, for if we are to succeed in larger-order threshold crossings—from the organic back into the inorganic, from life back into death—we will need all the reincorporative strength available to us. That strength will have only one source: entirety to ourselves and the infinite appetite to make it real.

Testimony and Threshold

When asked where something is, we often respond by *pointing*.
Charles Hockett, *Animal Sounds and Communication*

Finally we return to where we began, to the issue raised by untranslatability. We have persistently negated this negative concept and replaced it with argument or evidence—leading to the conviction that we can know and feel all. The intelligible world has yielded mutual conversions among zones as seemingly twain as those of Coleridge and Carnap or as rhetorically distant from one another as the descriptive strategies of Char and Origen. We have seen granite and mind interact into sculpture and—under the same onto-logical duress—the harsh *relicta* of Kuaua refuse to refuse us their trace of our personality. It has seemed in place—by flights of both volition and consistency—to reclaim *in potentia* the very geology from which the Face in the Mountain was cut. There was behind all this—I shamelessly repeat—the weaponry of logic, and yet I think the argument was spared either the aridity of logic or the solipsistic self-reference with which, say, Schelling managed to reclaim all data for the "I." And there has been one specific reason for whatever richness adheres to our logical principle. That "specific reason" is the subject of this essay.

There has been at least implicit, in all the foregoing, the notion that when a threshold is crossed, a testimony goes up. (Didn't an artesian fountain spring into the air at the touch of Pegasus' hoof?) Testimony has appeared here as the sound or clarification of threshold crossing, and yet I have made no effort to account for this alleged bond, this identity as close as that between lightning and thunder.

In one of my first essays, "From Naming to Fiction Making,"[1] I traced the origins of language to love, to a desire in the namer to draw the nameable world up into himself, to hold it carefully. I see that, unpremeditatedly, the present work takes a similar route. Naturally enough, however—with that greater complexity which is aging's tax—I see more difference and mediation in the act by which mind appropriates things and situations in their names. It seems that the primitive-generative naming act is a way in which we translate the other into ourselves, proclaiming if often dubiously an identity that we alone can guarantee, yet nevertheless proclaiming it, shouting it out in its name. The name—*rose, chihuahua, incarnadine*—becomes our cry of qualification at the once-again-nonunity between ourselves as consciousness and the appearance the other insists on presenting to us; the name becomes the sound of the threshold.

Thus the act of naming exemplifies the process by which we instinctively testify to our discovery of the new. Naming is the model for threshold crossing, and testifying to it? But then why in naming do we so testify? Why do we emit the word as *signum*?

The answer—here and implicitly throughout this book—must lie in the anatomy of recovery and recuperation. There must be that, in the mind-work by which we reacquire ourselves as named totality, from which testimony as such springs. If we can find that element in mind-work we will come close to the bond between the liminal and testimony.

Let's take this turn of argument back into the genesis of language.

When we emit the name by which we let the thing bind itself to us we emit that small blurt of astonishment—that half-shaped *bowwow* or *purple* or *moon*—which signals our recovery of a part of ourselves. Originally (and I mean this literally) we are parts of the whole world—by implication, by intuition, by brute participation. The infant knows nothing, and everything, by inherence in the human situation encased in the global situation. His or her total consciousness implicitly knows its existence-place and the thereness of its *realia*. Part of ourselves as infants, the world we wish to recover later in life, is in fact ours for the being at the outset. It is that world at the recovery of which we are forever emitting the nuanced gasp that is language.

(Interlude for the concrete. I—at this writing—spend every morning working in my office with a presently three-and-a-half-month-old infant, my daughter Carson. I wonder at the power of a baby to draw us—me, my colleagues, passersby—back into her, to take us out of ourselves into her self envisaging us. Or are we simply taken back into her enduring us, into the complexities and compromises she lets us see we are? Whichever account comes true, I have to believe Carson preexists the great split of consciousness off from its objects. We search, through her, for the oneness our self-divisiveness promises as its overcoming of itself. We testify in this search to our sense of what she sees that we do not see.)

Nuanced gasp? The phonologist—talking of fricatives and glottal stops and soft palates—reminds us through what chunky machinery our response to world recovery must move; and once again we thrill at the friction between consciousness and its objects—soul and body. Still the raw sound of awareness, with which the *infans* greets our naming invitation, is already from its start a positing of distinctions and syntax. The prenap burble is part of creative shaping, a refining of the language-emitting powers. The gasp will become nuanced, losing as it does (in the majority of adults) all but its power to divide up the one whole world; and in fallen language (the vulgar of commercialism) losing even that power. Even at that, however, the language of the daily remains for the adult a privileged zone of nostalgia, the act most effectively excavatable toward the memory of oneself as hunger for the world and testimony to that hunger.

Naming provides the instances in this last essay, where I palp for bonds between threshold crossing and testimony. That flash of new awareness which goes with the giving of names is a primal threshold crossing for us, setting in with the *infans*—the still-nonspeaker—and growing identical with that hunger for the new, for that connection seeing and connection seeking which is in us the only path to growth.

The essays in this book have dealt with threshold crossings—which in fact are these essays themselves. In that sense the essay on the essay was a paradigm for the other pieces. That essay was written as the teaching of a class, thus invented itself through the discussions of what it itself was. (The writing down of that essay, which I managed in the week intervening between class meetings, was part of the class, as the class was part of the essay—and the whole effort served as a prolonged gasp of wonder, a testimony.) It fitted this essay that it concerned and tried to anatomize a genre of writing that was itself occasional, always already. . . .

In a looser sense, every essay in this book, and the book as a whole, illustrates the same spring-tense proximity of new awareness, thresholds of consciousness, and the impulse to testimony. I retreat in thought to the geneses of the two longest essays, those on water and imagination. Neither essay began from the desire to investigate, to inquire into the other as distinctly separated object. (That long vaunted goal of humane scholarship was borrowed from the proclaimed ideals of the physical sciences and is of questionable use in either domain.) "The Quanta of Imagination" sprang from. . . . (I pause. Why not be honest? The threads that weave out into this essay are filaments from many ovipositors . . . dust out into the air from different directions, from different times.) That essay rolled into place from within my desire to sustain the Romantic view of imagination—which lies close to my collective dream-sources—while assuring myself of its tougher endurances. Oversimplified though this account is, it explains my line of argument; that in its genesis text-thinking creates, and uses while discovering, the objects of its attention, the building blocks of its discourse. This is a sense in which we are instructed by the new, but the guiding motifs and determining telos are hidden from the start in the self that instigates.

(Fine distinctions, to make room for the new in this fundamentally Platonic account of anamnesis. The testimony of surprise, which I claim to hear in the world-recuperating act of naming—is it surprise at the new or the pure shock of recognition? How could man see the sun if he were not the sun already? I propose a worldview in which the authentically new—the advance in medicine, the freeing of new artistic style, the effective innovation in political economy—is that because it understands, with new deepness, what the old is doing with itself and on what line the curve of human time is arching back toward its origins.)

"The Argument of Water" is also an argument of self with self—and in its way the same argument as that on imagination. The narrator of the essay lives a conflict of choices, the split-apart languages by which the same element can be named. (He can trace in himself a dominant awareness: all the speech on the globe reduces to a single meaningful sound. Or he is walking at noon through a large city and watching millions of passing faces, and each of them—in symbiosis with him—is straining to become a single articulate expression.) The inward convergence of the intelligible draws him, as do the many-hued disguises the lady wears. Furthermore—and here is where the conquering restlessness of the self recurs—he longs to know what the language of analysis will say to confirm the language of his dreams (as in studying imagination he longs to know himself as wholeness, through the widely separated expressions of him that other people are).

Historical time serves as the proving ground for the points made here about threshold crossing and testimony. One of my essays deals with a limited time sector, the past century and a half, but the rest survey a somewhat more spacious calendar: Thales to Roethke, Snyder to Catullus, Addison to Tom Wolfe. What relevance has the temporal to the syntax of naming, threshold crossing and recuperation, and finally testimony—that syntax which I have taken as theme of this book?

The human temporal dimension is as real as a lap, and no more. It is there when you sit down and look around, then gone when you stand and walk forward. When you are sitting, the lap— or the history of mankind—is definingly substantial. The apparent firmness of time derives from this: that it provides an explanatory context, semantic filler, in terms of which to read texts, artifacts, or events. (Marxist historiography is as off as Toynbee's in its belief that the social-historical is an explanatory matrix for human significance.) In the present essays I have turned chronology upside down—as in the seventh, where I drove toward the past and tracked it to its mythical lair in the present. In both strategies I have been filling and packing around meaning.

But of course there is more, intimately apposite, to say of time's ingredience with the events central to this book. The pathos of temporality—fictitious though it is—is itself the sound of the cry of testimony, gasp of recognition or bleat of defeat. Time is in this sense what makes us express ourselves, though it is only our creation. In crossing thresholds we recuperate lost parts of ourselves, and in so doing recognize again what has been temporarily cut from us and what we have just regained. That recognition is an intimate awareness of time's passing—which discloses itself in an instant that wipes time out. Recognition of that stripe is what gives birth to testimony, to the kinds of calling attention to new synthesis that this book is. The sound of testimony, naturally, is the sound of the soft palate, but in this production spirit is identical with the will of the cells. A sound goes off in the soul at the impulse of the recognized, and the tragicomedy of infinite replay is once more enacted inside us. The problem of the new—of both its inevitability and its impossibility—is raised here freshly, as is that note of joyful terror with which we salute the infinite limitation of our knowing power.

Notes

Untranslatability

1. Heine, *"Seraphine,"* pt. 10, in *Sämtliche Werke,* vol. 1, *Gedichte* (Munich, 1969) 247.
2. Roberts and Jenness, *Canadian Arctic Expedition 1913–1918,* vol. 14 (Ottawa, 1925) 332.
3. Goodwin, *First Lessons in Manx,* 3d ed. ([Peel, Isle of Man], 1966).
4. *Genesis* 11:4–9.

Beauty As the Threshold of Nature with Art

1. Will, *Intelligible Beauty in Aesthetic Thought* (Tübingen, 1958).
2. Will, *Literature Inside Out* (Cleveland, 1966).
3. Stokes, *The Stones of Rimini* in *The Critical Writings of Adrian Stokes* (London, 1978) 1:193.
4. Ibid. 196.
5. Ibid. 219.
6. Ibid. 231.
7. Ibid. 235.
8. Watson, *Behaviorism* (New York, 1970) 248.
9. Winckelmann, *Werke* (Donaueschingen, 1808) 61.
10. Goethe, *Sämtliche Werke: Jubiläums-Ausgabe* (Stuttgart & Berlin, 1902–7) 30:110.
11. Ibid. 27:264.
12. Ibid. 35:325.
13. Ibid. 34:17.
14. Marcel, *Homo viator,* trans. Craufurd (Chicago, 1951) 213–70.
15. Rilke, *Duino Elegies,* trans. Leishman and Spender (London, 1948) 87–88.
16. Ibid. 83.
17. Maritain, *Creative Intuition in Art and Poetry* (New York, 1955) 126.
18. Ibid. 138.

19. Brecht, "Chance-Imagery," in *The Discontinuous Universe,* ed. Sears and Lord (New York, 1972) 93.
20. Heisenberg, "The Representation of Nature in Contemporary Physics," in *Discontinuous Universe,* 127.
21. Sontag, "The Aesthetics of Silence," in *Discontinuous Universe,* 50–75.
22. Derrida, "Structure, Sign, and Play," in *Writing and Difference,* trans. Bass (Chicago, 1978) 279.
23. Foucault, "What Is an Author?" in Harari, *Textual Strategies* (Ithaca, 1979).

The Argument of Water

1. Brice Parain, *Recherches sur la nature et les fonctions du langage* (Paris, 1940).
2. "The Lao Tzu (Tao-te ching)," sec. 8 in *A Source Book of Chinese Philosophy,* ed. and trans. Chan (Princeton, 1963) 143.
3. *The Vedanta-Sutras with the Commentary by Sankarakarya,* trans. Thibaut, Sacred Books of the East, vol. 38 (Oxford, 1896) 107–8.
4. Thales, frag. 3, in *Die Fragmente der Vorsokratiker,* ed. Diels (Hamburg, 1957) 11–12.
5. Pindar, *Olympian Odes* 1.1–3, in *The Odes of Pindar,* trans. Lattimore (Chicago, 1947) 1.
6. Meng-tsu, in *The Sacred Books of Confucius and Other Confucian Classics,* ed. and trans. Chai and Chai (New Hyde Park, NY, 1965) 97.
7. *Shayast lashayast* 15, 28 in *Pahlavi Texts,* trans. West, Sacred Books of the East, vol. 5 (Oxford, 1880) 378.
8. "The Story of Sumedha," secs. 24–25, in *Buddism in Translations,* ed. and trans. Warren (Cambridge, 1922) 6–7.
9. *The Teaching of Buddha,* nos. 44–51 (Tokyo, 1934).
10. From *The Sutra of 42 Sections,* trans. Ch'an (London, 1947).
11. M. Lidzbarski, *Das Johannesbuch der Mandäer* (Giessen, 1915) 56, 216.
12. Hans Jonas, *The Gnostic Religion* (Boston, 1958) 97–98, 39, respectively.
13. *Clementine Homilies* 8.17, Ante-Nicene Christian Library, vol. 17 (Edinburgh, 1870) 145.
14. 1 Peter 3:18–21.
15. Tertullian, De baptismo 9, in *Tertulliani opera* pt. 1, Corpus christianorum: Series latina, vol. 1 (Turnhout, 1954) 283–84.
16. Ibid. 284.
17. Origen, *Tractatus de libris sanctarum scripturarum,* ed. Battifol (Paris, 1900), Tractatus XV, pp. 165–66.
18. Chrétien de Troyes, *Le Roman de Perceval,* ed. Roach (Geneva, 1956) lines 2994–3023.
19. Robert de Boron, *Le Roman de l'estoire dou Grael,* ed. Nitze (Paris, 1927) lines 2660–70.
20. Aristotle, *Meteorologica* 3, 11, 378c.
21. Pseudo-Lully, cited in Read, *Prelude to Chemistry* (London, 1936) 148. Details on original source not given.
22. Bonnellus, *La Turbe des philosophes qui est appellé le code de vérité en l'art,* in *Trois traitez de la philosophie naturelle,* ed. Arnauld (Paris, 1618).

23. Melchior Ciboniensis, cited in Canseliet, *Alchimie* (Paris, 1964) 189.

24. Newton, *The Correspondence of Sir Isaac Newton* (1668–1694) (Cambridge, 1961) 3:210, 211.

25. Rouhault, *System of Natural Philosophy* 3.3 (London, 1723) 2:132.

26. Boyle, *Works* (London, 1672) 3:309.

27. Leeuwenhoek to Huygens May 26, 1676, Observations II and III, cited in Schierbeek, *Measuring the Invisible World* (London, 1959) 62–63.

28. Bacon, *Works of Francis Bacon* (Philadelphia, 1851) 2:94.

29. Stevens, "The Glass of Water," in *Collected Poems* (New York, 1957) 197–98.

30. Roethke, "Meditation at Oyster River," in *The Far Field* (New York, 1964) 17.

31. T. S. Eliot, "The Dry Salvages," in *Four Quartets* (New York, 1943) 21–22.

32. James Joyce, *Ulysses* (New York, 1946) 655–56.

33. René Char, *Hypnos Waking,* trans. Jackson Mathews (New York, 1956) 201, 233, 239.

The Quanta of Imagination

1. Ryle, *The Concept of Mind* (New York, 1949).

2. Ibid. 27.

3. Ibid. 248.

4. Ibid. 260–61.

5. Ibid. 266.

6. Ibid. 270.

7. Black, "Metaphor," in *Philosophy Looks at the Arts,* ed. Margolis (New York, 1962).

8. Ibid. 227.

9. Ibid. 234.

10. Wheelwright, *Metaphor and Reality* (Bloomington, 1962).

11. Ibid. 172.

12. Ibid. 72–73.

13. Ibid. 78.

14. Wittgenstein, *Tractatus logico-philosophicus* (London, 1963).

15. Stenius, *Wittgenstein's Tractatus* (Ithaca, 1964).

16. Derrida, *Glas* (Paris, 1974).

17. Russell, *Logic and Knowledge* (London, 1956) 223.

18. For further discussion of these intricacies, consult Russell, *The Philosophy of Logical Atomism and Other Essays, 1914–1919* (London, 1986).

19. Carnap, *The Logical Structure of the World* (Berkeley, 1967).

20. Ibid. xi.

21. Ibid. 311.

22. Ibid. 325.

23. Ibid. 329.

24. Geach-Black, *Translations from the Philosophical Writings of Gottlob Frege* (Oxford, 1980) 60.

25. Ibid. 61.

26. Frege, "The Thought," *Mind* 65(1956): 295.

27. Ibid. 294.

28. Ibid. 294–95.

29. Carnap, *Logical Structure,* 326.

30. Ibid.

31. C. D. Broad, "The Local Historical Background of Contemporary Cambridge Philosophy," *British Philosophy in the Mid-Century* (London, 1957) 15.

32. Cited in J. Pucelle, *L'idéalisme en Angleterre* (Neuchatel, 1955) 19.

The Essay As Threshold

1. Lukács, "On the Nature and Form of the Essay," in *Soul and Form* (Cambridge, MA, 1974).

2. Selzer, *Confessions of a Knife* (New York, 1979).

3. Adorno, "Der Essay als Form," in *Noten zur Literatur I* (Frankfurt, 1958) 9–49.

4. Montaigne, "Of the Cannibals," in *Essays of Michael, Lord of Montaigne,* trans. Florio (London, 1910) 1:214–15.

5. Addison, *Spectator* vol. 4, no. 275, in *The Spectator* (London, 1924) 2:90.

6. Lamb, "A Dissertation upon Roast Pig," in *The Essays of Elia and Eliana* (London, 1926) 156.

7. Pater, "Leonardo da Vinci," in *The Renaissance* (London, 1914) 125.

8. Wolfe, "The Kandy-Kolored Tangerine-Flake Streamline Baby," in *The Kandy-Kolored Tangerine-Flake Streamline Baby* (New York, 1965) 76–77.

Limits in the Time of Consciousness

1. Will, "Shamans in Turtlenecks," *New Literary History,* 13(1982): 411–19.

2. Snyder, "A Walk," in *The Back Country* (New York, 1968).

3. In Adorno, "Rede über Lyrik und Gesellschaft," in *Notem zur Literatur I* (Frankfurt, 1958) 73–104.

4. Alfred de Vigny, "La Mort du Loup," in *Oeuvres Complètes de Alfred de Vigny: Poésies* (Paris, n.d.) 222–25.

5. Will, *The Fact of Literature* (Amsterdam, 1972).

6. Angelus Silesius, *Angelus Silesius, Cherubinischer Wandersmann* (Paris, 1946) 2:53; 1:287, 204, respectively.

7. Villon, *Le Grand Testament* 86 (New York, 1967) 56.

8. Horatius Flaccus, *Carmina,* I:28. The translation is by C. E. Bennett.

9. Sappho, Epithalamion I App., in *Poetarum Lesbiorum Fragmenta,* ed. Lobel and Page (Oxford, 1968) 86. Version mine.

Testimony and Threshold

1. Will, "From Naming to Fiction-Making," *Giornale di metafisica* 5(1958): 569–83.

Frederic Will lives in Iowa with his wife, who is a flutist, and two small children. His earlier books include *Literature Inside Out* (1966), *Our Thousand Year Old Bodies* (poems, 1980), and *Shamans in Turtlenecks* (selected essays, 1984). He is presently completing a volume on the American trucker's experience of space.

The manuscript was edited by Michael K. Lane. The book was designed by Joanne E. Kinney. The typeface for the text and the display is Galliard. The book is bound in ICG Arrestox Linen.

Manufactured in the United States of America.